Spotlight on Reading

A teacher's toolkit of
instant reading activities

Glynis Hannell

Routledge
Taylor & Francis Group

LONDON AND NEW YORK

First published 2009
by Routledge
2 Park Square, Milton Park, Abingdon, Oxon OX14 4RN

Routledge is an imprint of the Taylor & Francis Group, an informa business

© 2009 Glynis Hannell

Typeset in Sabon by
Florence Production Ltd, Stoodleigh, Devon
Printed and bound in Great Britain by
MPG Books Ltd, Bodmin

British Library Cataloguing in Publication Data
A catalogue record for this book is available from the British Library

ISBN10: 0–415–47307–1 (pbk)
ISBN13: 978–0–415–47307–1 (pbk)

Contents

Other books from Routledge by Glynis Hannell

Spotlight on Language: A teacher's toolkit of instant language activities
978–0–415–47311–8

Spotlight on Writing: A teacher's toolkit of instant writing activities
978–0–415–47308–8

Spotlight on Spelling: A teacher's toolkit of instant spelling activities
978–0–415–47305–7

Spotlight on Your Inclusive Classroom: A teacher's toolkit of instant inclusive activities
978–0–415–47306–4

Success with Inclusion: 1001 Teaching strategies and activities that really work
978–0–415–44534–4

Dyscalculia: Action plans for successful learning in mathematics
978–1–84312–387–3

Dyslexia: Action plans for successful learning
978–1–84312–214–2

Promoting Positive Thinking: Building children's self-esteem, self-confidence and optimism
978–1–84312–257–9

CHAPTER 1

Introduction

Reading: a skill for life

Reading is, of course, a critically important skill for all pupils. Reading is a key element for inclusion, within the classroom, family, community and workplace.

Pupils who read well can participate to the full in the classroom programme. Good readers can experience the interest and enjoyment that reading can bring and they can participate in a range of social, community and leisure activities where reading is needed. As they get older they can further their education or their vocational skills and more readily gain employment.

Poor reading skills

On the other hand, poor reading inevitably places a substantial barrier between the individual and many of life's opportunities. In our community we can see only too clearly how poor reading skills result in social and economic disadvantage and severely limited employment choices.

In the classroom, lack of adequate reading ability poses a strong risk that the pupil will not be fully included in the learning experiences that are on offer.

Pupils who experience reading difficulties may become very disheartened and have limited expectations for their own success. These disenchanted pupils are often unsettled and poorly motivated in the classroom, to the detriment of their own and others' learning.

Your inclusive classroom

An effective classroom literacy programme will take into consideration the needs of pupils who may need individualised materials, explicit teaching and opportunities for extended practice to build their skills. An inclusive approach to the teaching of literacy delivers a double advantage to pupils. First, a flexible, inclusive approach will mean that all pupils with receive appropriate teaching and make the best progress possible. Second, the advantages of good reading skills will filter into every aspect of the pupils' lives, in school and beyond.

If classroom instruction fails to be sufficiently inclusive and appropriate to the pupils' needs, the pupils' reading skills will fail to develop and the cycle of disadvantage and negativity increases. However, when success is experienced, confidence, interest, motivation and enjoyment often follow.

Reading is a complex skill and it follows that many pupils in your classroom will need a high level of effective, inclusive teaching, over an extended period of time, in order to be able to reach a reasonable level of competence.

Reading is a complex process

Have you ever stopped to think what a remarkable process occurs as young pupils learn to read? If you have, it will come as no surprise to find that many pupils have to work hard to master this complex, multifaceted skill.

The human brain has to negotiate many hurdles in order to be able to read successfully. Two, quite separate, areas of the brain will both need to develop specialist skills and then unite to perform a new, integrated skill that we call 'reading.'

The visual areas of the brain will need to learn to recognise sequences of printed letters as familiar patterns. The eyes will have to develop the physical skills of scanning along lines of print. While this is happening the language centres of the brain will need to acquire skills in processing sequences of sounds and understanding the meaning of the printed language.

These two quite different systems then have to interface in a seamless fashion. Information that is first received as intricate visual patterns will need to be translated into sounds and words that can be understood just as easily as spoken words. For competent reading to occur these complex processes have to be successfully linked together in a continuous, fluent stream.

Reading is a high-order language skill, in which comprehension, interpretation and response are also critically important components of the process that we call 'reading'.

Let us look at how this book, *Spotlight on Reading*, connects with the basic building blocks of reading and enables you, the teacher, to provide effective, inclusive teaching for all your pupils.

Spotlight on Reading: foundations of success

Phonics and phonological awareness

Pupils need a clear understanding of how printed words relate to speech patterns before they can make progress with reading. This capacity is recognised as a fundamental building block for reading.

The ability to decode printed letters into language equips pupils with a powerful tool to develop their own reading, independent of adult help. Pupils who lack skills with phonics are excluded from this 'self help' way of reading.

Chapter 2 provides a range of reading activities to promote phonological awareness and skills in using phonics. Real and nonsense words are used to promote your pupils' ability to use phonics to decode a range of words.

Whole words

Although phonics is of the utmost importance in the development of reading skills, the English language also contains irregular, exception words that pupils will not be able to *sound out*. These words will need to be taught in a different way.

Did you know that the list of the most commonly used 100 words contains some of the most difficult *exception* words? Words are difficult to learn if they:

- are abstract;

- look like other abstract words.

The, *he*, *there*, *here* and *her* are typical examples of difficult exception words.

On the other hand, words are easy to learn if they:

- are visually distinctive and easily distinguished from other words;

- are interesting or meaningful.

Spaghetti, *tyrannosaurus* and *tsunami* are good examples of words that are easy to read!

Chapter 3 provides activities to promote your pupils' recall of 'difficult to remember' words, activities to promote their observation skills in detecting small differences between words, and some fun activities for learning unusual and interesting sight words too.

Reading comprehension

The skills involved in reading comprehension are complex. Pupils' underlying ability to understand language in general, spoken or written, will be pivotal in their learning. If a pupil has a limited vocabulary or has difficulties in understanding sentence structure, then, whether the language is written or spoken, the pupil will be at risk of poor comprehension.

Reading comprehension also involves thinking and reasoning. Often this has to be more abstract than the type of logic that is required in practical, everyday situations.

Chapter 4 will help your pupils to work on the sub-skills of reading comprehension. Discriminating between good and inadequate answers, locating specific information and formulating good answers are included in the range of comprehension activities introduced in Chapter 4.

Reading practice

The ability to read fluently and accurately generally evolves from quite a lengthy period of development, in which the young pupil is building skills in automatic word recognition and speedy, internal word decoding.

It is unrealistic to expect a pupil to pick up a book and read it aloud without preparation or rehearsal. Even as skilled, adult readers, we would often request some time to prepare before we read anything unfamiliar in public. Just like learning any new skill, practical rehearsal of reading produces gains in performance.

Frequent repetition helps to build a permanent link between the printed word and language. Instead of the slow process of careful word decoding, the pupil can use a much more efficient process of rapid, internal word decoding and/or automatic word recognition. The more words that the pupil can read automatically, the more fluent and meaningful the pupil's reading will become.

Chapter 5 gives your pupils varied opportunities to rehearse a reading task. The reading is shared between several readers (including the teacher if this works best), so that a higher level of interest can be introduced, without overloading individual readers.

Effective, inclusive teaching

Let us briefly look at some of the key elements of effective, inclusive teaching:

- Teacher and pupils talk, explore, discuss and work on reading together.

- There are lots of opportunities for pupils to learn from each other.

- The teacher provides individual assistance when pupils need this.

- Every pupil can participate in the same type of activity.

- Classroom activities are individualised to meet pupils' differing skill levels.

- Extra support and scaffolding are given when pupils need them.

- Stereotypes do not limit individual pupils' opportunities.

- All pupils have the chance to take on new challenges and extend themselves.

- Pupils are taught how to think about reading.

- Pupils are taught reading and learning strategies.

- Sub-skills of reading are taught to all pupils.

- Teaching is explicit and focused.

- Understanding is developed through examples, discussion and explanation.

- All pupils have sufficient practice to master what they have been taught.

- Mistakes or incorrect answers are viewed as valuable teaching opportunities.

- Reading activities engage the pupils' interest.

- Activities offer disadvantaged pupils enrichment as well as skills.

Spotlight on Reading in your inclusive classroom

Differentiated learning materials for inclusion

Each of the activities in this book is presented at three levels of difficulty. Level 1 is the easiest level, Level 2 intermediate and Level 3 the most difficult. There is deliberate overlap between the three levels to allow for easy transitions between one level and the next.

One activity can be used to suit a wide range of pupils within a mixed ability class. For example, a teacher may use Level 2 for most of the class, but direct the more able pupils to continue on with Level 3 items, while their younger or less able classmates work on Level 1 items. All pupils will be doing exactly the same activity, but at different levels of difficulty.

The gradual increase in difficulty levels and the overlap between levels helps teachers to provide *inclusive activities* in their classrooms.

Pupils with language or learning difficulties

The graded difficulty levels within each activity allow the teacher to allocate appropriate *differentiated tasks* to a wide range of pupils, so that everyone can be included in the same activity, at varying levels, according to their ability.

Pupils who experience difficulty with reading may benefit from introductory work on an easier level than some other pupils. This is often sufficient to prepare them to cope with the more *challenging* items that follow. The teacher can make a decision on whether to:

- provide additional teaching support to help the pupil complete the activity; or

- if the first level is successfully completed, have the pupil progress to the more difficult levels of the same activity; or

- if the first level has only been completed with assistance, have the pupil move to a similar activity, but at the same level of difficulty as before and provide assistance as required on the new activity.

For example, Jack and Jill have both been given Level 1 of *Which word will be in the answer?* (Activity 15) from Chapter 4 on 'Reading comprehension'.

Jack coped with this quite easily, so the teacher decides that he can now move on to Levels 2 and 3 of this same activity.

Jill, however, clearly found Level 1 quite challenging, so she is not yet ready for the more difficult Level 2. Instead, the teacher provides more support by using Level 1 as a teaching tool and spending time talking to Jill about each item in turn. In doing so the teacher provides extra *scaffolding* and *support* for Jill.

The teacher might also use this *explicit teaching* technique the next time Jill has a reading comprehension activity drawn from another publication. The teacher might also create a similar activity based on the curriculum that the class is following. This provides Jill with fresh learning materials and further opportunity to work in this area of reading.

Throughout the book, teachers will find opportunities to provide additional input and assistance when this is needed.

A key principle for inclusive teaching is that teachers vary the amount and style of support given to pupils of varying abilities. For example, while one pupil may be able to answer a question without any prompts or hints, another may need the teacher to give more scaffolding and assistance such as:

- discussion

- leading questions

- helpful comments, hints or clues

- multiple choice options.

For example, if Daisy cannot find the word that matches the clue *A long thin animal*, her teacher might say '*Look, there are two animals here, the frog and the snake. Which do you think is the long thin one?*' The resultant learning is still valid, but has required more structure to achieve the end result.

Pupils with advanced development

The more advanced pupils often gain considerable insight into a task by participating in the easier items, in which the *thinking* processes and the *strategies* used are usually more concrete and overt.

For example, in *Finding whole words* (Activity 8), the strategy of working by a process of elimination may be more obvious at the easier levels but readily reapplied at the more difficult level.

Pupils who have advanced reading development usually thrive on activities that challenge them. Teachers can readily select a range of activities and/or levels to provide the bright pupil with *individualised activities* that will extend their reading skills. For example, a very advanced six-year-old might start with Level 2 of the selected activity and even move through to Level 3 if able to do so.

Interactive, inclusive and explicit teaching

Unlike many other pupil workbooks, *Spotlight on Reading* activities are intended to be used as *explicit* teaching materials, and as the basis of *interaction* between teacher and pupil(s). Teachers may often find that the younger and less able pupils benefit from participating in classroom *discussion* and attempts at the more difficult levels. Classroom interaction and discussion will give them good models for successful completion of the activities. This provides an opportunity for the pupils to be *challenged* and perhaps to break a *stereotype* of what they can and cannot do.

Reading is a complex skill and many pupils will benefit from working on *sub-skills*, so that small facets of reading are explicitly taught and practised in a supportive learning environment. Throughout this book teachers will find activities that focus on a targeted sub-skill of reading.

For example, in *Reading detective* (Activity 17), the pupils, with their teacher's support, discover how to find the clues that give information to the reader. The word *her* in the sentence *Goldie fell asleep in her warm basket* tells the reader that Goldie is female, while the word *deck* in the phrase *tumbling wildly across the deck* tells the reader that the characters in the story are on a boat.

All the activities can generate useful discussion and interaction between pupils and teacher (or helping adult) in a small group or one-to-one setting. For example, the activity *Listen and say the answer* (Activity 19) already has a clear set of prompts for the pupils. However, good teaching opportunities will still occur.

Seven-year-old Gerald has listened to the teacher read a passage about butterflies and has been asked the question '*What does a chrysalis look like?*' He has used the prompt, *A chrysalis looks . . .* and has given the answer '*A chrysalis looks brown.*' The teacher can agree that his answer is factually correct, but then show him how to refer back to the text to support his answer, which would then be '*A chrysalis is brown and looks like a curled-up dead leaf.*'

Similar opportunities for promoting reading skills by *discussion*, *coaching* and *support* occur throughout this book.

Reading: a key skill for life

Through every age and stage of life reading provides information, stimulation, learning and enjoyment. These classroom activities, which all promote reading, will provide your pupils with opportunities to develop skills that will serve them well throughout their lives.

Users' guide to *Spotlight on Reading*

Ethical and inclusive teaching

All the reading activities in this book have been carefully written to provide teachers with ethical, responsible and inclusive teaching materials. Although the main purpose of each item is to promote the development of your pupils' reading skills, the materials also promote social responsibility, personal resourcefulness and thoughtfulness towards others.

The use of language related to popular culture (such as superheroes and fantasy), the supernatural, specific religious beliefs or inappropriate role models has been avoided.

Flexibility

Teachers can draw activities from any section, in any order, according to the needs of a particular group of pupils. For example, a teacher may want to concentrate on phonics and so may use several of the activities from Chapter 2, 'Phonics' (Activities 1–6) in quick succession. Another teacher may be aware that some pupils have limited reading comprehension skills and so decide to draw on the activities in Chapter 4, 'Reading comprehension' (Activities 13–19).

Ease and speed of use

The book is ready for instant teaching. The only preparation required is for the teacher to preselect the appropriate activity for the class, group or individual.

The activities provide a variety of valuable reading experiences that can form the basis of a single lesson or series of lessons.

These activities are often quick to do and ideally suited to short sessions, where one or more levels of items can be given to the class as a whole, or a selected group of pupils, as required. Many activities are also perfect for a quick, intensive burst of reading when there are only a few minutes to spare.

Teaching notes

The teaching notes at the start of each activity provide teachers with a brief rationale for the activity and practical teaching hints. In some situations suggested correct answers, sample answers and guides are provided for the teacher's convenience.

Suitability for parents or teaching assistants

Teachers may find that parents will welcome the activities in this book for fun-based learning at home. The teaching notes also enable paraprofessionals or even volunteers (such as parents assisting in a learning support programme) to use the activities designated by the pupil's teacher.

Suitability for classroom, small group or individual lessons

The activities in this book all lend themselves to classroom, small group or individual lessons, in which pupils and teacher work on the items collaboratively. The varied nature of the activities allows teachers to select those that can form the basis of an individualised programme for a particular pupil or group of pupils with special needs.

All the activities are intended to provide pupils with explicit teaching of the key sub-skills of reading. As such, they are suitable for pupils with special needs as well as mainstream pupils. The teacher can adjust the degree of individual guidance and support according to the needs of the pupils he or she is working with.

Supplementing a remedial programme

While the book is not intended as a specialist reading programme, teachers and others working with pupils can use the activities as supplementary work to be done at home and at school.

An emphasis on language

Reading is a high-order form of language and we cannot separate it out from other forms. You will find that, while many activities throughout this book do require the pupils to read, many can be adapted or used as oral language activities. This is particularly useful when working with pupils with limited reading skills. Being able to complete a task as an oral language activity is a great foundation for the reading skills that will come later. It also means that the pupil can be fully included in the classroom activity, but can work with the activity in oral rather than written form.

For example, if eight-year-old Jake is still at a very early stage of reading, he may still be able to complete and really benefit from *Compound words* (Activity 5) as an oral language activity. Understanding how words such as *fingernail* or *pineapple* are made up of two smaller words will stand him in good stead as his reading skills advance.

Teachers are encouraged to use all the activities as the basis for classroom discussions. The activities also offer many opportunities for teachers to follow through with further development, perhaps in written work or curriculum-based reading activities.

Oral reading

Of course, all the activities are primarily reading tasks, but this does include oral reading as well as silent reading.

Many of the activities do have a built-in oral reading component, for example *Word pairs* (Activity 3) needs the teacher to read the first word in a pair and the pupil to read the second. All the activities in Chapter 5, 'Rehearsed reading' (Activities 20 to 25) are oral reading exercises. Oral reading is the route through which the teacher can hear and understand how the pupil is coping with reading tasks and where any problems are occurring.

Emphasis on print not illustrations

Illustrations are not used to support pupils' reading in this book. Why is that? The reason is simple. In this book we are helping pupils to use printed words. We want to encourage the pupils to focus on the print and to do this we keep illustrations in the background, so that the pupils depend on the print itself.

Worksheets

Although the activities are primarily intended for reading work with oral responses, the book has been set up so that teachers may, if they wish, copy any activity for their pupils to use as a worksheet. Teachers are given permission to copy any activity for use with the pupils that they teach.

Teachers can identify different levels of difficulty, or different volumes of work. For instance, one pupil might be asked to attempt only Level 1, or the teacher might circle the specific items in an activity that the pupil is required to complete. Alternatively, the teacher may set a given number of items to be completed, for example 'Choose any six questions from this sheet.'

Teachers of pupils with special needs may find it useful to work through the activity with the pupil on one worksheet and then use a clean copy of the worksheet for the pupil to work through the same task again independently.

Making connections

All learning works best if it is connected with other learning. The exchange and cross-fertilisation of emerging skills that occur within a classroom can create a powerful network of interlinked learning.

The activities in this book are specifically directed at reading, but teachers will find that they can create links with writing, spelling, spoken language and other incidental and formal reading activities that occur within the classroom.

For example, the class may have worked on *Reading detective* (Activity 17), which the teacher then links into a writing activity:

> Remember how we found a word that gave us a clue when we were reading? When you write your story can you use a word that gives a clue about how Sam was feeling?

Follow-on activities

The activities are carefully constructed to provide pupils with appropriate reading activities. Many teachers will find it useful to devise other, similar activities on current classroom topics, using the activities in this book as a model. For example, *Nonsense words* (Activity 1) provides practice in decoding real and nonsense words using phonics. A teacher could easily make up similar lists to reinforce any new sounds being taught. The pupils could even make up their own lists of real and nonsense words using their new sound.

Approximate age levels

There are no hard and fast rules about which particular activities should be given to children of a particular age or reading level. The activities are flexible and open to teachers to use in a variety of ways with a wide range of ages and abilities.

However, the chart below gives a guide to the approximate levels that are usually appropriate for different reading ages.

Indication of levels appropriate for given reading ages			
Reading age	**Level 1**	**Level 2**	**Level 3**
5.5 to 6.5 years	**Usually quite easy**	**Likely to present some challenges**	**Likely to be very challenging**
	Some teacher support may be needed	May work well as an oral language activity for some pupils Pupils will need some teacher support	May work well as an oral language activity for some pupils Pupils will need a high level of teacher support
6.5 to 8 years	**Easy**	**Usually quite easy**	**Likely to present some challenges**
	Good for consolidation and practice of basic skills Good for explicit teaching of strategies and techniques before moving on to the more difficult levels	Some teacher support may be needed	May work well as an oral language activity for some pupils Pupils will need some teacher support
8+ years	**Very easy**	**Usually quite easy**	**Likely to present some challenges**
	Good for pupils who need a high level of explicit teaching and support despite reasonably adequate reading skills	Good for consolidation and practice of basic skills Good for explicit teaching of strategies and techniques	May work well as an oral language activity for some pupils Pupils will need some teacher support

CHAPTER 2

Phonics

Patterns and relationships

Written language is a very ingenious system. Using only 26 letters of the alphabet, we can create an almost infinite number of words simply by combining and recombining those letters in a variety of different patterns. If words were just visual patterns without any underlying system, we would have to remember thousands and thousands of different word patterns by rote.

The ability to 'sound out' words is fundamental to the development of reading skills. Readers of all ages draw on their knowledge of the letter–sound associations and the rules that govern the ways in which sounds interact. For example, you can probably read the words *moatate* or *bullacle* without too much difficulty, even though you have never seen these words before. You can do this because you have the ability to reuse knowledge you already have to build up an accurate version of these new words.

For young readers the development of the skills required to work out words using sounds is a complex and lengthy process. First, they have to learn the sounds of the letters. But, as any expert reader knows, single letters combine in different ways to give different sounds: *o* in *hot* sounds different from *o* in *oat*; *c* in *cat* sounds different from *c* in *chat* or *peace*.

Not only do pupils have to be able to give the correct sounds accurately to the letters they see, they also have to have adequate phonological awareness to allow them to recognise the relationship between a string of sounds, for example, *w-it-ch* and the word *witch*.

In all aspects of learning, being able to think about your own thinking and processing is a powerful strategy in advancing your skills. Throughout this chapter you will find opportunities to talk to your pupils about *how* they thought things through and *what* they did. Being able to explain and talk about the strategies used, for instance in changing a word by substituting one sound for another, significantly enhances the pupils' ability to work intelligently with print.

Activity 1: Nonsense words

Teaching notes

Pupils' skills in using phonics are exercised in *Nonsense words*. The introduction of nonsense words shows the pupils how to apply their knowledge of one word pattern to another, very similar word. This ability to apply knowledge of existing words quickly and flexibly to new and, as yet, unfamiliar words is one of the essentials of reading. Pupils will gain skills and, more importantly, confidence in their own abilities, by finding that they can read words that do not even exist!

Level 1 works with simple onset–rime patterns. The nonsense words are created by manipulating the initial consonant sounds that precede simple vowel–consonant (or double consonant) word endings.

Level 2 introduces words endings that include a vowel blend (such as *oa*) and also demonstrate the use of the *final e*. Consonant blends are also introduced as initial sounds to increase the challenge for the pupils.

Level 3 introduces more complex, and less familiar word endings and includes some of the more difficult initial letter combinations, such as *pn* and *qu*.

Some pupils will need their teacher to model the task or you may need to give individual pupils help to get started.

There are no teacher's charts for this activity.

Activity 1

Nonsense words

LEVEL 1

Here are some real words and some nonsense words, all mixed up together. See if you can read all the words.

1	**pet**	wet	fet	yet	zet	ket	vet
2	**pill**	will	yill	bill	vill	hill	lill
3	**hot**	not	fot	cot	jot	pot	zot
4	**well**	yell	mell	tell	rell	sell	vell
5	**bug**	fug	kug	mug	yug	pug	gug
6	**tap**	rap	bap	lap	zap	kap	dap
7	**sick**	lick	bick	tick	mick	jick	pick
8	**nest**	best	hest	pest	fest	jest	dest
9	**pig**	tig	kig	mig	fig	wig	dig

Activity 1

Nonsense words

LEVEL 2

Here are some real words and some nonsense words, all mixed up together. See if you can read all the words.

1	**best**	west	nest	fest	dest	hest	test
2	**pink**	wink	kink	tink	plink	stink	smink
3	**boat**	coat	toat	swoat	skoat	float	stoat
4	**room**	boom	poom	broom	soom	loom	croom
5	**bite**	mite	kite	pite	clite	phite	swite
6	**race**	face	trace	skace	drace	place	mace
7	**peach**	beach	reach	neach	deach	teach	sneach
8	**dirt**	firt	skirt	shirt	slirt	tirt	wirt
9	**coin**	poin	groin	join	boin	troin	ploin

 From: *Spotlight on Reading*, Routledge © Glynis Hannell 2009

Activity 1

Nonsense words

LEVEL 3

Here are some real words and some nonsense words, all mixed up together. See if you can read all the words.

1	**fight**	tight	jight	chight	splight	kight	twight
2	**team**	beam	shream	weam	queam	pheam	stream
3	**riddle**	giddle	middle	fiddle	niddle	spriddle	whiddle
4	**joint**	point	foint	troint	pnoint	swoint	floint
5	**ridge**	fidge	plidge	bridge	hidge	midge	swidge
6	**bakes**	flakes	twakes	prakes	stakes	pakes	sprakes
7	**lawn**	rawn	prawn	kawn	trawn	brawn	hawn
8	**coach**	toach	broach	joach	skoach	troach	noach
9	**fudge**	hudge	smudge	budge	studge	kudge	pludge

Activity 2: Nonsense sentences

Teaching notes

In *Nonsense sentences* the pupils are asked to read a sentence and detect the word that is incorrect. To do this they will have to:

- make an accurate phonic decoding of each word in the sentence;
- think about what the sentence is really meant to say;
- exchange the incorrect letters and replace them with letters that restore the correct sound into the word.

You may also find it useful to ask the pupils to:

- Explain what was wrong with the sentence. Recognising a word that looks and sounds wrong in a sentence is an important reading skill that helps the pupil to self-correct when reading.
- Explain what they had to do to remedy the error and how this worked. For

example, a pupil might say '*"Lits" is not a real word; it is supposed to be "lots". But "lots" has the "o" sound in the middle, not "i". So I took out the "i" and put the "o" in instead, then the word said "lots".*' Giving this explicit account helps the pupil to formulate a clear understanding of the process and demonstrates meta-awareness of the system used to represent speech sounds in print.

Level 1 deals with simple, consonant–vowel–consonant words.

Level 2 deals with words that include the *final e*, vowel–consonants and vowel blends.

Level 3 deals with words that include vowel blends embedded in more complex words.

There are no teacher's charts for this activity.

Activity 2

Nonsense sentences

LEVEL 1

In each sentence one word is wrong. Change the letters in the word so that the sentence makes sense.

1 My log likes to go for a walk.

2 On my birthday I have lits of fun and a cake.

3 The boys in the park pan over to the ducks.

4 Toast and honey is very hummy.

5 On Monday I did a good jog for my teacher.

6 Put the things in the bog and post it.

7 If you give your friend a hug they will hut you back.

8 You can write your name with a pin.

9 The little birds were safe in their best.

Activity 2

Nonsense sentences

LEVEL 2

In each sentence one word is wrong. Change the letters in the word so that the sentence makes sense.

1 The dinosaurs lived a pong time ago.

2 You can light the lump when it is dark.

3 The cat hints mice.

4 Can you smell the word dinosaur?

5 Pump up your boke tyres and go for a ride.

6 There were some fir trays in the forest.

7 You can oat rice with chopsticks or a spoon.

8 Have you soon the new picture in the library?

9 There was a steam at sea and the ship was wrecked.

From: *Spotlight on Reading*, Routledge © Glynis Hannell 2009

Activity 2

Nonsense sentences

LEVEL 3

In each sentence one word is wrong. Change the letters in the word so that the sentence makes sense.

1 Beat the eggs up with a brisk and then make an omelette.

2 If you exercise a lot you will become very wrong.

3 The band had a fuddle player and a drummer.

4 People sometimes squirt in bright light.

5 A train can have several couches as well as an engine.

6 The bus stepped at the school to collect the pupils.

7 The boat was sealing across the lake in the breeze.

8 The pointer mixed up a lot of colours before he started the picture.

9 Elephants can lean to do tricks if they are taught by a good elephant trainer.

From: *Spotlight on Reading*, Routledge © Glynis Hannell 2009

Activity 3: Word pairs

Teaching notes

If you were faced with the new word *ixygen* you would, in all probability, recognise its similarity to the word *oxygen*. Then you would be able to take a short cut to reading the new word. Mentally you will have engaged in a process of 'phoneme substitution', by replacing one sound with another.

Many young pupils do not use this strategy or realise its potential for helping them with new words. How often have you listened to a pupil painstakingly 'sounding out' a word that is almost identical to one that they already know.

In *Word pairs* the pupils have the opportunity to hear one word and instantly to read another word, using phoneme substitution. The activity can be used as a teaching opportunity in which pupils and teacher can discuss the way that words are transformed by changing just one letter or phoneme.

In Levels 1 and 2 only initial and middle sounds are manipulated. In Level 3 final sounds are also included to extend the pupil's range.

There are no teacher's charts for this activity.

Activity 3

Word pairs

LEVEL 1

 Listen to your teacher read the first word in the row, then you read the second word.

	Teacher	You
1	cat	rat
2	pig	dig
3	mad	sad
4	neck	peck
5	tall	wall
6	best	nest
7	pack	pick
8	tick	tock
9	mice	rice

Activity 3

Word pairs

LEVEL 2

 Listen to your teacher read the first word in the row, then you read the second word.

	Teacher	You
1	rule	mule
2	stop	step
3	stick	stock
4	chalk	stalk
5	field	shield
6	grade	glade
7	squeeze	sneeze
8	grain	drain
9	whale	scale

Activity 3

Word pairs

LEVEL 3

 Listen to your teacher read the first word in the row, then you read the second word.

	Teacher	You
1	explain	complain
2	wrench	quench
3	laundry	launch
4	fewer	skewer
5	pleasure	treasure
6	typhoon	typhoid
7	anxious	noxious
8	design	resign
9	vogue	rogue

Activity 4: Crazy sentences

Teaching notes

As we know, words can often be grouped according to their endings. For example, *pig*, *wig* and *big* share the same ending or *rhyme*. Once pupils can recognise and read commonly used word endings, they become more efficient readers because they can deal with several letters as a familiar cluster of sounds, instead of a series of single letters.

One stumbling block for many young readers is that they do not scan the words ahead to look for these familiar clusters of letters. To teach this skill, in *Crazy sentences* the pupils are given explicit directions to:

- scan ahead to find the target word(s) that contain a given *rhyme*;
- read the sentences that include the *rhymes*.

The sentences are 'crazy' because, although they are grammatically correct and make some sort of sense, they do not allow the pupils to rely on context cues to predict the next word. The pupils are pretty much forced to rely on using their phonic knowledge to read the sentences. By repeating the same word ending several times in each sentence, pupils have practice in applying it to several words, some of which may be unfamiliar or unexpected. The repeated exposure to a particular rhyme also helps to develop the pupils' ability to read words containing that rhyme automatically without having to rely on overt 'sounding out'. (The 'sounding out' process still occurs, but at an internal and eventually subconscious level.)

Teachers working with pupils on this activity may like to have them pronounce the rhyme before they begin to scan the sentence for words containing that set of letters.

There are no teacher's charts for this activity.

Activity 4

Crazy sentences

LEVEL 1

Here are some rhymes and some sentences. Look at each rhyme and find all the words that end in that rhyme in the sentence. Draw a circle around the words and then read the sentence.

	Rhyme	Sentence
1	am	Pam and Sam put jam on ham.
2	eg	Meg has a peg on her leg.
3	ell	Yell! The bell fell in the well.
4	oss	Toss the moss at the boss.
5	op	Pop can hop on top of a mop.
6	ill	Jill will get a bill for the pill.
7	og	My dog and hog can jog on a log.
8	ig	A big pig in a wig did a jig on a fig.
9	et	I bet the vet will let my wet pet go in a jet.

From: *Spotlight on Reading*, Routledge © Glynis Hannell 2009

Activity 4

Crazy sentences

LEVEL 2

Here are some rhymes and some sentences. Look at each rhyme and find all the words that end in that rhyme in the sentence. Draw a circle around the words and then read the sentence.

	Rhyme	Sentence
1	ing	The king said bring me a ring on a string.
2	uck	The duck got stuck in the back of the truck.
3	ink	A pink mink can drink but not blink.
4	ock	It's a shock to find a mock rock in your sock.
5	ake	Wake in the lake and shake yourself dry.
6	ole	The mole and the vole stole the whole pole.
7	ook	The cook had a look at the book on the hook.
8	oe	'Woe,' said Joe, 'I hit my toe with the hoe.'
9	ibble	My baby can dribble and nibble and scribble.

From: *Spotlight on Reading*, Routledge © Glynis Hannell 2009

Activity 4

Crazy sentences

LEVEL 3

Here are some rhymes and some sentences. Look at each rhyme and find all the words that end in that rhyme in the sentence. Draw a circle around the words and then read the sentence.

	Rhyme	Sentence
1	**oat**	The goat in the boat had a coat that would float.
2	**owl**	An owl can howl, growl and scowl.
3	**ew**	Few of us flew with the crew we knew.
4	**etch**	Fetch the sketch for the wretch in the ketch.
5	**eigh**	Weigh the sleigh or the horse will neigh.
6	**awl**	Crawl and then sprawl on the shawl but don't bawl.
7	**ouch**	Don't be a grouch or slouch on the couch.
8	**eak**	The freak gave a weak squeak at the top of the peak.
9	**east**	The beast had a feast on yeast in the east.

Activity 5: Compound words

Teaching notes

Being able to break words into sections is a useful skill – it often transforms what might be a long and difficult word into a series of short, manageable syllables. Pupils often need explicit teaching and guided practice to realise that, when they look at a word, they can often find familiar groups of letters. Even if they cannot immediately read the syllable, they may discover that the syllable is very easy to *sound out*. When at least one syllable has been recognised or decoded, the second syllable and the whole word often falls easily into place. For example, a pupil may be puzzled by a word such as *cupcake*. However, once *cup* has been worked out, the task of reading the whole word is not so difficult after all.

One of the easiest ways to introduce the skill of using syllables is to use *Compound words* that are composed of other, real words, rather than abstract syllables. This makes the recognition of the separate components of a word much easier.

In Level 1 the words used have at least one short, consonant–vowel–consonant word within them. In Level 2 the words have more complex patterns, with both syllables containing at least one letter blend, such as *ch*, *oo* or *th*, or using a final *e* or *y*. In Level 3 the complexity of the words is again increased by introducing letter sequences such as *ough* and *ight*.

Encourage your pupils to become observant when they read. There are many interesting compound words in everyday reading, and finding them can really increase reading skill and confidence.

There are no teacher's charts for this activity.

Activity 5

Compound words

LEVEL 1

Here are some words for you to read. Look carefully and you will see two little words in each word. Draw circles around each of the two little words first and then read the whole word.

1 popcorn

2 peanut

3 jigsaw

4 kidnap

5 ladybug

6 jellyfish

7 mailbox

8 cupcake

9 doormat

Activity 5

Compound words

LEVEL 2

Here are some words for you to read. Look carefully and you will see two little words in each word. Draw circles around each of the two little words first and then read the whole word.

1 chopstick

2 butterfly

3 hairbrush

4 airport

5 baseball

6 bathroom

7 armchair

8 earring

9 driveway

From: *Spotlight on Reading*, Routledge © Glynis Hannell 2009

Activity 5

Compound words

LEVEL 3

Here are some words for you to read. Look carefully and you will see two little words in each word. Draw circles around each of the two little words first and then read the whole word.

1 breakfast

2 earthquake

3 pineapple

4 fingernail

5 pickpocket

6 doughnut

7 brainstorm

8 floodlight

9 frostbite

Activity 6: Rhymes for fun

Teaching notes

Rhymes for fun presents some humorous rhymes for pupils to read. The rhymes reinforce phonic patterns and help to develop the pupils' understanding of how words relate to each other. Of course, the rhythm in the verses also helps to enhance the pupils' awareness of the speech patterns they are working with.

As well as being enjoyed as light-hearted reading experiences, the verses can also be used for teaching purposes.

Here are the verses used and details of the particular aspect of reading practice each one provides.

Level 1

Three little pigs
Practises the *ot* rhyme or word ending.

Grandpa's hat
Practises the *at* rhyme or word ending.

Level 2

My funny bunny
Practises the *y* word ending.

Tilly, Milly and little Billy
Extra practice for the *y* word ending.

Eat your bready
Extra practice for the *y* word ending.

Peas and pies
Practises *ea* and *ie* sounds.

Level 3

Square eyes
This verse presents a range of rhyming patterns and provides the teacher with opportunities to talk with the pupils about words that rhyme but that do not share the same spelling pattern, for example *said* and *bed* or *care* and *there*.

Activity 6

Rhymes for fun

LEVEL 1

Read these little poems out loud.

Three little pigs

Three little pigs
Said with a grin
We will not not not
Let you in

Three little pigs
Got got got
The big bad wolf
In their pot pot pot

Ow yow
It's hot hot hot
Sitting in this
Pot pot pot

Grandpa's hat

The bat, the cat and the big fat rat
All sat under Grandpa's hat
Bat, rat and big fat cat
Don't you know you can't do that?

Activity 6

Rhymes for fun

LEVEL 2

Read these little poems out loud.

My funny bunny

It's funny my bunny likes honey
It's funny my bunny likes jam
It's funny my bunny likes noodles
It's funny she really hates ham

Tilly, Milly and little Billy

Tilly, Milly and little Billy
Socks on their heads
They do look silly

Eat your bready

Ready, steady
Eat your bready
If you don't
You'll soon be deady

Peas and pies

I don't like peas
I don't like pies
Baby bear just cries and cries
No peas? No pies?
Said mother bear
Then you will go to bed
No peas! No pies!
Said baby bear
And put them on his head

From: *Spotlight on Reading*, Routledge © Glynis Hannell 2009

Activity 6

Rhymes for fun

LEVEL 3

Read this little poem out loud.

Square eyes

You'll get square eyes
Oh yes you will
That's what my mother said
Square eyes I thought
Now that's a change
And lay down on my bed

Square eyes would look unusual
But really I don't care
I'd see all sorts of lovely things
I didn't know were there!

Square eyes would be fantastic
Just think of how they'd look
My eyes would fit the pages
If I had to read a book

I'd see in all the corners
Square eyes sound good to me
And all I have to do to get them
Is to watch and watch TV.

CHAPTER 3

Reading whole words

Instant recognition

Throughout this book you will find many activities that help your pupils to develop good phonic skills so that they can *sound out* unfamiliar words. As professional teachers we all know that sounding out is an essential foundation reading skill.

However, in this chapter you will find activities to develop skills in reading *whole words* automatically, without the need for sounding out.

So why, after placing so much emphasis on phonics and sounding out, do we have a chapter on whole words? Why do pupils need to be able to read whole words at sight?

Some words occur over and over again in print and it is very useful to be able to read these words instantly, without the need to sound out. This skill (called *automaticity*) is an important element in skilled, fluent reading. Instant recognition of whole words speeds up the reading process, helping to maintain the sense of what is being read.

Nearly every child finds it easy to recognise words such as *elephant* or *spaghetti* because these words are visually distinctive, so in this chapter, for both fun and confidence building, we introduce some whole words that have high interest and visual appeal.

On the other hand, words such as *was* or *have* are visually unremarkable and abstract and can be very difficult to remember, so in this chapter extra practice is provided in reading some of the difficult to remember, but commonly used, words.

But a more pressing reason for these activities is the fact that some words in the English language are irregular and do not sound out. These words can be confusing for pupils who are learning to read, who may have been told time and time again to *sound it out* when they need to read an unfamiliar word. Then they come to a word such as *once* and sound out o-n-c-e. Or they encounter *who* and say the sounds w-h-o. These words are, of course, irregular. They do not follow the accepted patterns of phonics and are therefore potentially very frustrating for the pupil who is trying to learn how to read.

Another cluster of words that do not sound out as expected are those taken from another language, such as French. Many pupils understandably stumble over words such as *plateau* or *antique*, which have unexpected letter sequences and unfamiliar pronunciations.

Activity 7: Reading whole words

Teaching notes

Reading whole words is intended to be interactive, with the teacher (or other adult) and pupil working together. The activity gives pupils practice at recognising and reading whole words. The words are taught in context, making it much easier for the pupils to 'connect' with these quite abstract words.

The steps in this activity are:

- *Step 1: The pupil is asked to read a single word in isolation*

This can be challenging as the pupil has to rely on recognising or sounding the word out, without the benefit of context cues. In many instances the teacher will need to give help, telling the pupil the single word.

- *Step 2: The pupil then finds the target word in the adjacent sentence*

Once again help may be needed. For example, the teacher may need to read the whole sentence to the pupil, encouraging the pupil to follow the words and find the target word. The teacher should give as much help as required.

- *Step 3: The pupil is asked to read out the whole sentence*

In some situations it is helpful if the teacher reads the whole sentences first, as a model, and then asks the pupil to reread the sentence once the teacher has finished.

If the pupil initially sounded the target word, it is appropriate at this stage to encourage them to shift to whole word reading. Prompts such as '*Just say the word*' can be given.

- *Step 4: The pupil is asked to reread all the target words again, from the chart at the bottom of the worksheet*

The teacher should give as much help and support as necessary. Sentences can be read again and again, and the words on the chart read several times over if the teacher judges that this is a useful exercise for the pupil. The aim is for the pupil to be able to read all the sentences and the words on the chart quickly and confidently.

There are no teacher's charts for this activity.

Activity 7

Reading whole words

LEVEL 1

You will see a word and then a sentence. Read the word by itself and then find the word in the sentence. Then read the sentence.

1 you   I will give you a birthday present.

2 they   Sam and Ben said they had fun.

3 with   I like to play with my little dog.

4 have   You can have two cookies.

5 this   'Did you make this mess?,' said Mom.

6 what   What will the naughty monkey do next?

7 very   A hippo can run very fast.

8 was   The elephant was stuck in the mud.

9 are   Look! There are three tigers in my bed.

Now see if you can read the words again.
Your teacher will tick ✓ the words you get right.

	✓		✓		✓
very		this		with	
was		you		are	
have		what		they	

From: *Spotlight on Reading*, Routledge © Glynis Hannell 2009

Activity 7

Reading whole words

LEVEL 2

You will see a word and then a sentence. Read the word by itself and then find the word in the sentence. Then read the sentence.

1 right If you get all of these right you are very smart.

2 before Look before you jump into a lake.

3 does A lion does not like to eat pancakes.

4 through Can you get through the keyhole?

5 about Did I tell you about the day I flew to the moon?

6 many There are so many stars that you cannot count them.

7 their Dolphins look after their babies and teach them tricks.

8 would If you lived on the moon it would be very lonely.

9 were Once upon a time there were three little pigs.

Now see if you can read the words again.
Your teacher will tick ✓ the words you get right.

	✓		✓		✓
about		their		right	
many		does		were	
before		would		through	

From: *Spotlight on Reading*, Routledge © Glynis Hannell 2009

Activity 7

Reading whole words

LEVEL 3

You will see a word and then a sentence. Read the word by itself and then find the word in the sentence. Then read the sentence.

1	**earth**	Dinosaurs walked on the earth before man.
2	**while**	You have to wait while the lights are red.
3	**certain**	You have to make certain there are no alligators in the pool.
4	**unusual**	It is very unusual for dogs to dance.
5	**unique**	You are unique; there is no one else exactly like you!
6	**language**	Aliens might speak in a strange language of their own.
7	**weigh**	A hippo can weigh up to 800 pounds.
8	**column**	If you take away the column the roof will fall in.
9	**original**	If you write a new song it is an original.

Now see if you can read the words again.
Your teacher will tick ✓ the words you get right.

	✓		✓		✓
earth		while		weigh	
language		original		unique	
column		unusual		certain	

From: *Spotlight on Reading*, Routledge © Glynis Hannell 2009

Activity 8: Finding whole words

Teaching notes

In *Finding whole words* pupils are asked to match single words with sentences that give a definition or explanation of the word. At each level there are nine words to be matched.

Working with the target words will help the pupils to build a repertoire of words that they can read independently. However, the sentences may also challenge the pupils' reading skills, because there are some quite difficult words embedded in the sentences.

This is intentional and the interaction between teacher and pupil will be important in making the best use of this activity.

Thinking, vocabulary and reading skills may all be developed as the pupils use reading, trial and error and a process of elimination to make a perfect set of matched words and sentences.

Here are the charts of target words and answers.

Level 1

Word	Sentence number
boat	2
friend	6
snake	7
aeroplane	9
frog	5
sun	8
huge	3
snow	4
clown	1

Level 2

Word	Sentence number
many	3
double	5
city	4
change	7
voice	8
eight	6
closed	2
answer	9
globe	1

Level 3

Word	Sentence number
desert	5
opposite	4
instant	9
proper	8
pneumonia	3
segment	7
continue	1
telepathy	6
tsunami	2

Activity 8

Finding whole words

LEVEL 1

Read each sentence and find the word that matches.
Put the sentence number in the box next to the word.

1   A funny person.

2   Another name for a ship.

3   This means very, very big.

4   This is white and very cold.

5   A green animal that lives in water.

6   Someone you play with.

7   A long, thin animal.

8   This shines in the sky.

9   This can fly.

boat		aeroplane		huge	
friend		frog		snow	
snake		sun		clown	

Now see if you can read the words. Your teacher will tick ✓ the words you get right.

	✓		✓		✓
boat		aeroplane		huge	
friend		frog		snow	
snake		sun		clown	

From: *Spotlight on Reading*, Routledge © Glynis Hannell 2009

Activity 8

Finding whole words

LEVEL 2

Read each sentence and find the word that matches.
Put the sentence number in the box next to the word.

1 A round map of the world.

2 The opposite of open.

3 This means lots and lots.

4 A very big place where a lot of people live.

5 Two things; exactly the same.

6 A number that comes after seven.

7 To make something different.

8 You use this to sing and talk.

9 You give this when you are asked a question.

many		change		closed	
double		voice		answer	
city		eight		globe	

Now see if you can read the words. Your teacher will tick ✓ the words you get right.

	✓		✓		✓
many		change		closed	
double		voice		answer	
city		eight		globe	

From: *Spotlight on Reading*, Routledge © Glynis Hannell 2009

Activity 8

Finding whole words

LEVEL 3

Read each sentence and find the word that matches.
Put the sentence number in the box next to the word.

1 To keep on doing something.

2 A huge wave in the sea caused by an earthquake.

3 An illness that affects your lungs.

4 Totally different; at the other end.

5 A very dry part of the world.

6 The ability to read someone else's mind.

7 A section or piece of something.

8 Correct; the right thing to do.

9 Immediate; happens right away.

desert	☐	proper	☐	continue	☐
opposite	☐	pneumonia	☐	telepathy	☐
instant	☐	segment	☐	tsunami	☐

Now see if you can read the words. Your teacher will tick ✓ the words you get right.

	✓		✓		✓
desert		proper		continue	
opposite		pneumonia		telepathy	
instant		segment		tsunami	

From: *Spotlight on Reading*, Routledge © Glynis Hannell 2009

Activity 9: Word detective

Teaching notes

In *Word detective* the pupils have to find pairs of words that look slightly different from each other. This demands good whole word recognition and accurate visual discrimination. Then the pupils have to read the sentences and decide which one makes

sense. This combines skills of word recognition, word decoding and reading comprehension.

Here are the teacher's charts with the correct word underlined.

Level 1		
1	one	<u>on</u>
2	boot	<u>boat</u>
3	<u>mud</u>	mug
4	<u>how</u>	who
5	when	<u>where</u>
6	bog	<u>dog</u>
7	<u>father</u>	feather
8	house	<u>horse</u>
9	free	<u>tree</u>

Level 2		
1	bread	<u>beard</u>
2	<u>king</u>	knight
3	muddle	<u>middle</u>
4	lump	<u>lamp</u>
5	tried	<u>tired</u>
6	poodles	<u>noodles</u>
7	<u>skimmed</u>	skinned
8	<u>pebbles</u>	peddles
9	revolver	<u>revolves</u>

Level 3		
1	trail	<u>trial</u>
2	violent	<u>violin</u>
3	<u>certain</u>	curtain
4	crown	<u>crowd</u>
5	curse	<u>course</u>
6	<u>sequel</u>	equal
7	<u>stranger</u>	stronger
8	<u>released</u>	rehearsed
9	properly	<u>property</u>

Activity 9

Word detective

LEVEL 1

Read each pair of sentences. Find the differences and circle the words. Then tick ✓ the sentence that makes sense.

1 I jumped on the bed and hit my head.
I jumped one the bed and hit my head.

2 The pirate boot sailed around the island.
The pirate boat sailed around the island.

3 Jack fell in the puddle and got mud on his face.
Jack fell in the puddle and got mug on his face.

4 Can you show me how to make a cake?
Can you show me who to make a cake?

5 Tell me when the teacher put my hat.
Tell me where the teacher put my hat.

6 My bog is a poodle called Buster.
My dog is a poodle called Buster.

7 My father painted the kitchen with yellow paint.
My feather painted the kitchen with yellow paint.

8 The boys had a ride on the big house.
The boys had a ride on the big horse.

9 The birds made a nest in the free in the forest.
The birds made a nest in the tree in the forest.

From: *Spotlight on Reading*, Routledge © Glynis Hannell 2009

Activity 9

Word detective

LEVEL 2

Read each pair of sentences. Find the differences and circle the words. Then tick ✓ the sentence that makes sense.

1 The old man had a long white bread and rosy cheeks.
The old man had a long white beard and rosy cheeks.

2 The king and queen's daughter was a beautiful princess.
The knight and queen's daughter was a beautiful princess.

3 The island was in the muddle of the dark blue lake.
The island was in the middle of the dark blue lake.

4 It was so dark that they had to light the lump immediately.
It was so dark that they had to light the lamp immediately.

5 Sally was so tried that she fell asleep on the train.
Sally was so tired that she fell asleep on the train.

6 I would like a huge bowl of poodles with fried chicken.
I would like a huge bowl of noodles with fried chicken.

7 The kids skimmed stones on the surface of the water.
The kids skinned stones on the surface of the water.

8 There were thousands of white pebbles on the beach.
There were thousands of white peddles on the beach.

9 The earth revolves around the sun once every 24 hours.
The earth revolver around the sun once every 24 hours.

Activity 9

Word detective

LEVEL 3

Read each pair of sentences. Find the differences and circle the words. Then tick ✓ the sentence that makes sense.

1 The judge said the trail would start on Monday.
   The judge said the trial would start on Monday.

2 The musician picked up his violent and started to play.
   The musician picked up his violin and started to play.

3 The clown was certain that there was a net to catch him.
   The clown was curtain that there was a net to catch him.

4 The whole crowd cheered when he won the race.
   The whole crown cheered when he won the race.

5 The athletes ran around the cross-country curse at top speed.
   The athletes ran around the cross-country course at top speed.

6 The book was so popular, everyone wanted a sequel.
   The book was so popular, everyone wanted an equal.

7 The stranger knocked at the door to ask the way to the town.
   The stronger knocked at the door to ask the way to the town.

8 The fisherman released the trapped fish from the net.
   The fisherman rehearsed the trapped fish from the net.

9 There were hundreds of umbrellas in the lost property office.
   There were hundreds of umbrellas in the lost properly office.

   From: *Spotlight on Reading*, Routledge © Glynis Hannell 2009

Activity 10: French words

Teaching notes

English incorporates words from several other languages, particularly French. These introduced words can challenge young readers, particularly with regard to unusual spelling patterns and unfamiliar pronunciations.

In *French words* it is assumed that a teacher will be working with the pupil(s) to help model the correct pronunciation of the words, and a pronunciation guide is given below. The words are introduced by simple, modelled reading.

Level 1

1	ballet	bal-ay
2	café	caf-ay
3	chef	sh-ef
4	crêpe	cr-ay-p
5	crèche	cr-esh
6	Mardi gras	Mar-dee gra
7	menu	men-yu
8	papier mâché	pap-ee-ay mash-ay
9	mousse	moo-s

Level 2

1	encore	on-cor
2	antique	an-teek
3	venue	ven-yu
4	forte	for-tay
5	Grand Prix	gr-on pree
6	debut	day-byoo
7	blonde	bl-on-d
8	bureau	bure-oh
9	chic	sh-eek

Level 3

1	en route	on-root
2	concierge	con-see-air-j
3	vinaigrette	vin-ay-gret
4	en suite	on sweet
5	à la carte	a la cart
6	art nouveau	art noo-voh
7	brunette	broo-net
8	cliché	cl-ee-shay
9	décor	day-cor

Activity 10

French words

LEVEL 1

 Listen to your teacher read the sentence, then you read it afterwards. Then read the French word on the right.

1 A ballet dancer can dance on her toes. <u>ballet</u>

2 You can buy food or drinks in a café. <u>café</u>

3 A chef can cook yummy food. <u>chef</u>

4 A crêpe is a sort of pancake. <u>crêpe</u>

5 They look after babies in a crèche. <u>crèche</u>

6 There are special parades at the
   Mardi gras. <u>Mardi gras</u>

7 The menu tells you what food you
   can order. <u>menu</u>

8 You can make things with
   papier mâché. <u>papier mâché</u>

9 Chocolate mousse is good to eat. <u>mousse</u>

Now see if you can read the French words by yourself.
Your teacher will tick ✓ the words you get right.

	✓		✓		✓
ballet		café		chef	
crêpe		crèche		Mardi gras	
menu		papier mâché		mousse	

From: *Spotlight on Reading*, Routledge © Glynis Hannell 2009

Activity 10

French words

LEVEL 2

 Listen to your teacher read the sentence, then you read it afterwards. Then read the French word on the right.

1 An encore is when the performer sings again.   <u>encore</u>

2 The antique car was very valuable.   <u>antique</u>

3 The pool was the venue for the party.   <u>venue</u>

4 Singing is not my forte.   <u>forte</u>

5 The motor champion won the Grand Prix.   <u>Grand Prix</u>

6 Sally made her acting debut in the school play.   <u>debut</u>

7 Her hair was very blonde.   <u>blonde</u>

8 He went to the information bureau.   <u>bureau</u>

9 She looked very chic in her new hat.   <u>chic</u>

Now see if you can read the French words by yourself. Your teacher will tick ✓ the words you get right.

	✓		✓		✓
encore		antique		venue	
forte		Grand Prix		debut	
blonde		bureau		chic	

Activity 10

French words

LEVEL 3

Listen to your teacher read the sentence, then you read it afterwards. Then read the French word on the right.

1   We can stop en route to Washington and have a meal.   en route

2   The concierge will give you a key.   concierge

3   Put vinaigrette on your salad   vinaigrette

4   There is an en suite bathroom.   en suite

5   Choose from the à la carte menu.   à la carte

6   Miami has some great art nouveau buildings.   art nouveau

7   My mother was a brunette when she was young.   brunette

8   'Raining cats and dogs' is an old cliché.   cliché

9   The décor of the room was very old fashioned.   décor

Now see if you can read the French words by yourself. Your teacher will tick ✓ the words you get right.

	✓		✓		✓
en route		concierge		vinaigrette	
en suite		à la carte		art nouveau	
brunette		cliché		décor	

From: *Spotlight on Reading*, Routledge © Glynis Hannell 2009

Activity 11: Interesting animals

Teaching notes

Although the names of animals may not necessarily occur frequently in reading materials, as a group of whole words they have a strong interest and appeal to young readers. The printed words are often visually distinctive, which makes them easy to remember. The words often conjure up images of the animals, which also helps the pupils to read the words next time they see them.

Some pupils may need the teacher's help in reading the sentences and the words.

Here are the teacher's charts of words and answers.

Level 1

Animal name	Sentence number
parrot	9
kangaroo	7
lion	6
chimpanzee	5
toad	8
elephant	2
dolphin	4
whale	3
giraffe	1

Level 2

Animal name	Sentence number
alligator	8
llama	3
walrus	5
hedgehog	2
koala	9
armadillo	7
orang-utan	6
wolf	4
squirrel	1

Level 3

Animal name	Sentence number
iguana	3
parakeet	4
cheetah	2
tortoise	5
piranha	9
chameleon	6
gnu	7
python	1
baboon	8

Activity 11

Interesting animals

LEVEL 1

Here are the names of some animals. Match the name of the animal with its sentence and write the sentence number in the box.

parrot	⬜	kangaroo	⬜	lion	⬜
chimpanzee	⬜	toad	⬜	elephant	⬜
dolphin	⬜	whale	⬜	giraffe	⬜

1 I am an animal with a very long neck.

2 I am the biggest animal on land.

3 I am the biggest animal in the sea.

4 I can swim and do tricks in the water.

5 I can climb and swing in the trees.

6 I roar very loudly.

7 I have my baby in my pouch.

8 I am like an ugly frog.

9 I am a bird but I can sometimes talk.

Now read the names of the animals out loud to your teacher, who will tick ✓ the ones you get right.

	✓		✓		✓
parrot		kangaroo		lion	
chimpanzee		toad		elephant	
dolphin		whale		giraffe	

 From: *Spotlight on Reading*, Routledge © Glynis Hannell 2009

Activity 11

Interesting animals

LEVEL 2

Here are the names of some animals. Match the name of the animal with its sentence and write the sentence number in the box.

alligator	☐	llama	☐	walrus	☐
hedgehog	☐	koala	☐	armadillo	☐
orang-utan	☐	wolf	☐	squirrel	☐

1   I hide nuts to eat in the winter.

2   I have a lot of prickles on my back.

3   I have long hair and four legs; I live in the mountains.

4   I am a sort of dog that lives in a pack.

5   I live in the sea and on land; I have long tusks.

6   I live in the forest; I am a primate.

7   I have armour on my back.

8   I have strong jaws and sharp teeth; I live in rivers and lakes.

9   I live in trees and eat gum leaves.

Now read the names of the animals out loud to your teacher, who will tick ✓ the ones you get right.

	✓		✓		✓
alligator		llama		walrus	
hedgehog		koala		armadillo	
orang-utan		wolf		squirrel	

Activity 11

Interesting animals

LEVEL 3

Here are the names of some animals. Match the name of the animal with its sentence and write the sentence number in the box.

iguana		parakeet		cheetah	
tortoise		piranha		chameleon	
gnu		python		baboon	

1 I am a type of snake that squeezes its prey.

2 I am an animal that can run very fast.

3 I am a large lizard.

4 I am a colourful bird.

5 I have a shell and move very slowly.

6 I can change colour when I need to.

7 I have horns; you can also call me a wildebeest.

8 I can swing from branch to branch in the trees.

9 I swim in rivers and, although I am small, I am dangerous.

Now read the names of the animals out loud to your teacher, who will tick ✓ the ones you get right.

	✓		✓		✓
iguana		parakeet		cheetah	
tortoise		piranha		chameleon	
gnu		python		baboon	

From: *Spotlight on Reading*, Routledge © Glynis Hannell 2009

Activity 12: Interesting food and drink

Teaching notes

Nearly all pupils are interested in what they eat and drink, and may sometimes be faced with a menu when they are away from home. The letter patterns associated with food and drink are often quite distinctive and quite easy to remember. Your pupils will be pleased to see how they can read these unusual looking words, and may even surprise their families if they stop for a meal on their next trip!

Some pupils will need the teacher to read the sentences and the words to them.

Here are the teacher's charts of words and answers.

Level 1

Food or drink	Sentence number
egg	8
spaghetti	5
milkshake	6
banana	1
hamburger	9
chocolate	7
peanut butter	2
apple	3
toast	4

Level 2

Food or drink	Sentence number
cornflakes	4
noodles	8
strawberry	6
doughnut	5
sandwiches	7
salami	9
pineapple	2
coffee	3
pizza	1

Level 3

Food or drink	Sentence number
nachos	8
sarsaparilla	6
lasagne	9
mozzarella	1
sushi	5
tangerine	7
artichoke	2
spinach	4
watermelon	3

Activity 12

Interesting food and drink

LEVEL 1

Here are the names of some types of food or drink.
Match the name of the food or drink with its sentence
and write the sentence number in the box.

egg	☐	spaghetti	☐	milkshake	☐
banana	☐	hamburger	☐	chocolate	☐
peanut butter	☐	apple	☐	toast	☐

1   This is a yellow fruit with a skin.

2   You can spread this on bread.

3   This is a round fruit; it has pips and skin.

4   This is bread that has been cooked.

5   This is a sort of pasta; it is long and thin.

6   This drink can be vanilla, chocolate or strawberry flavour.

7   This is used to cover biscuits or cakes; it is brown.

8   This can be cracked, and then you can fry it.

9   This has meat inside and bread outside.

Now read the names of the food or drink out loud to your teacher,
who will tick ✓ the ones you get right.

	✓		✓		✓
egg		spaghetti		milkshake	
banana		hamburger		chocolate	
peanut butter		apple		toast	

   From: *Spotlight on Reading*, Routledge © Glynis Hannell 2009

Activity 12

Interesting food and drink

LEVEL 2

Here are the names of some types of food or drink.
Match the name of the food or drink with its sentence
and write the sentence number in the box.

cornflakes	☐	noodles	☐	strawberry	☐
doughnut	☐	sandwiches	☐	salami	☐
pineapple	☐	coffee	☐	pizza	☐

1   This is usually covered with cheese and cooked in an oven.

2   This is a fruit that has a tough skin; it is yellow inside.

3   This is a drink for adults; they drink it black or with milk.

4   These are eaten at breakfast; they are golden yellow and crunchy.

5   This can be filled with jam or cream.

6   This is a sweet, red fruit.

7   These are made of two pieces of bread with a filling.

8   These are long, thin and usually white.

9   This is a type of Italian sausage.

Now read the names of the food or drink out loud to your teacher,
who will tick ✓ the ones you get right.

	✓		✓		✓
cornflakes		noodles		strawberry	
doughnut		sandwiches		salami	
pineapple		coffee		pizza	

Activity 12

Interesting food and drink

LEVEL 3

Here are the names of some types of food or drink.
Match the name of the food or drink with its sentence
and write the sentence number in the box.

nachos	☐	sarsaparilla	☐	lasagne	☐
mozzarella	☐	sushi	☐	tangerine	☐
artichoke	☐	spinach	☐	watermelon	☐

1 This is a type of cheese used on pizza.

2 This is a vegetable with tough leaves and a soft heart.

3 This is a large fruit, green outside and red inside.

4 This is a vegetable with dark green leaves.

5 This is a type of Japanese food with rice and fish.

6 This is a flavour for a cool drink.

7 This is an orange-coloured fruit with segments.

8 These are Mexican; they often have cheese on top.

9 This is a type of Italian pasta.

Now read the names of the food or drink out loud to your teacher,
who will tick ✓ the ones you get right.

	✓		✓		✓
nachos		sarsaparilla		lasagne	
mozzarella		sushi		tangerine	
artichoke		spinach		watermelon	

CHAPTER 4

Reading comprehension

Sub-skills for the fluent reader

This set of activities is all about explicit teaching of the sub-skills of reading comprehension. The exercises are *not* intended to be simple reading comprehension activities. Rather, they should be viewed as opportunities for the teacher and pupils to talk and learn about:

- *how* to set about the task of reading with understanding;
- *how* to demonstrate this understanding when responding to questions.

Reading comprehension involves a number of these critical sub-skills. First, of course, the pupil has to read both the text and the question accurately. To some extent this depends on actual reading capacity. However, general language and cognitive skills are also brought into play in comprehending what has been read. For example, *The man swallowed the fish* and *The fish swallowed the man* contain exactly the same reading vocabulary, but the order of the words transforms the meaning.

In many classroom, test and examination situations pupils have to read a passage and then produce acceptable written answers. In this there is an underlying requirement that the pupil not only understands the text itself, but also understands the question and can follow through and produce an answer. This answer has to be factually correct, but also has to relate to the specific question that has been asked. This linkage of text, question and answer is something that defeats many pupils, so specific attention is given to developing this skill in the activities that follow.

The chart on the following page contains the sub-skills exercised by the activities in this chapter.

Reading comprehension

Comprehension sub-skill	Activity number	Activity name
Extracting meaning	13	*Making sense*
Recognising similarities and differences in meaning	14	*Do they mean the same?*
Finding key words in the question and relating the answer to the key words	15	*Which word will be in the answer?*
Matching answers to questions and rejecting 'near miss' answers	16	*Choose the best answer*
Extracting the maximum information from the text by using inference and accurate interpretation of the language used	17	*Reading detective*
Listening and then formulating answers in complete sentences	18	*Listen and read the answer* (reading modelled answers)
Listening and then formulating answers in complete sentences	19	*Listen and say the answer* (formulating answers with the help of prompts)

Activity 13: Making sense

Teaching notes

A pupil may be able to read individual words with a high degree of accuracy, but may be quite devoid of understanding. To comprehend what is being read the pupil has to be able to connect with the meaning of the text as it emerges during the process of reading. Deciding whether a sentence *sounds right* (or not) places quite heavy demands on the pupil's language and cognitive skills.

In *Making sense* the pupil is asked to read a sentence and decide whether it makes sense or not. The deliberate errors in some of the

sentences relate to grammar and word use, not errors of fact. Teachers may be surprised to see how difficult some pupils find it to reject nonsensical sentences, indicating their underlying difficulty with the absolute fundamentals of reading comprehension. Teachers can talk to the pupils about how the incorrect sentences can be altered to make sense.

Here are the teacher's charts of sentences and answers.

Level 1

	Sentence	✓/✗
1	Sam is a good boy.	✓
2	The sun likes hot.	✗
3	Ann had a hat on her head.	✓
4	A pig is an animal big.	✗
5	The rat and the cat had on fight.	✗
6	Bess and Bill were twins.	✓
7	The baby fell up of her pram.	✗
8	My dog can do a lot of tricks.	✓
9	The man ran all the way to the town.	✓

Level 2

	Sentence	✓/✗
1	My mother is quite tall yesterday.	✗
2	My father is not as tall as my mother.	✓
3	The bugs buzzed aloudly.	✗
4	Too much ice cream can make you feel sick.	✓
5	Always remember to wipe your feet when they are muddy.	✓
6	The earth is round and unless beautiful.	✗
7	The nurse told the doctor in all the people were feeling better.	✗
8	Everyone at the show was given a huge bag of chips.	✓
9	He got to the top of the ladder and not could over the fence and into the road.	✗

Level 3

	Sentence	✓/✗
1	Bright Star was last in the race and knew that she could never silver.	✗
2	Dan squirted water all over the roof in an attempt to put the fire out.	✓
3	Harold used a special brush and comb to prepare Pooch for the dog show.	✓
4	Unfortunately too many to get into the boat that was only meant to hold twenty.	✗
5	The pirates sailed their ship up the river so that it could not be seen from the sea.	✓
6	Mrs Glad watched Kelly as she walked sadly away from the camp.	✓
7	Ever since Tammy was next year she had wanted to learn to dance.	✗
8	You are not permitted to enter unless you have a valid ticket.	✓
9	Luke switched on the television and began to a cartoon and eat a bag of popcorn.	✗

Activity 13

Making sense

LEVEL 1

Do these sentences make sense? Put a ✓ for **yes**, and a ✗ for **no**.

✓ or ✗

1 Sam is a good boy. _____

2 The sun likes hot. _____

3 Ann had a hat on her head. _____

4 A pig is an animal big. _____

5 The rat and the cat had on fight. _____

6 Bess and Bill were twins. _____

7 The baby fell up of her pram. _____

8 My dog can do a lot of tricks. _____

9 The man ran all the way to the town. _____

From: *Spotlight on Reading*, Routledge © Glynis Hannell 2009

Activity 13

Making sense

LEVEL 2

Do these sentences make sense? Put a ✓ for **yes**, and a ✗ for **no**.

✓ or ✗

1 My mother is quite tall yesterday. _____

2 My father is not as tall as my mother. _____

3 The bugs buzzed aloudly. _____

4 Too much ice cream can make you feel sick. _____

5 Always remember to wipe your feet when they are muddy. _____

6 The earth is round and unless beautiful. _____

7 The nurse told the doctor in all the people were feeling better. _____

8 Everyone at the show was given a huge bag of chips. _____

9 He got to the top of the ladder and not could over the fence and into the road. _____

Activity 13

Making sense

LEVEL 3

Do these sentences make sense? Put a ✓ for **yes**,
and a ✗ for **no**.

✓ or ✗

1   Bright Star was last in the race and knew that she
    could never silver.   _____

2   Dan squirted water all over the roof in an attempt to
    put the fire out.   _____

3   Harold used a special brush and comb to prepare
    Pooch for the dog show.   _____

4   Unfortunately too many to get into the boat that
    was only meant to hold twenty.   _____

5   The pirates sailed their ship up the river so that it
    could not be seen from the sea.   _____

6   Mrs Glad watched Kelly as she walked sadly away
    from the camp.   _____

7   Ever since Tammy was next year she had wanted to
    learn to dance.   _____

8   You are not permitted to enter unless you have a
    valid ticket.   _____

9   Luke switched on the television and began to a cartoon
    and eat a bag of popcorn.   _____

Activity 14: Do they mean the same?

Teaching notes

Do they mean the same? gives you, the teacher, an opportunity to show your pupils how to focus on subtle differences between sentences that, at first glance, seem to mean almost the same. Reading comprehension depends not only on reading accuracy but also on accurate cognitive and language processing, and this is what this activity is all about. Many pupils take what they read at face value and this often undermines accurate reading comprehension.

The explicit nature of the task also helps pupils to develop an awareness of the ways in which words and their position and usage can be used to manipulate meaning. This is a bonus for both reading comprehension and writing skills.

Be prepared to discuss the sentences with the pupils so that they understand how to reason using language, for example '*The first sentence says "use a broom" and the other sentence says "sweep". Those words mean the same thing. So the sentences mean the same too.*'

If you have used *Spotlight on Language: A teacher's toolkit of instant language activities*, you will already have used a similar activity called *Matching sentences* as an oral language exercise. The relationship between oral language comprehension and reading comprehension is, of course, very close, so the same activity is important in developing both skills.

The teacher's charts of sentences and answers arc on the following page.

Reading comprehension

Level 1

	Sentence 1	Sentence 2	✓/✗
1	I saw a fly on my pet bird	I saw my pet bird fly.	✗
2	Dad was angry with the dog.	Dad was mad at the dog.	✓
3	The boy bit the dog.	The dog bit the boy.	✗
4	Would you like cheese and crackers?	You are crackers to like cheese.	✗
5	Use a broom to clean the floor.	Sweep the floor with a broom.	✓
6	The milk was not cold.	The milk was hot.	✓
7	Nel gave her little sister a big hug.	Nel gave her big sister a little hug.	✗
8	Before you go to bed read a story.	Read a story then go to bed.	✓
9	Don't swing on the gate.	You must not swing on the gate.	✓

Level 2

	Sentence 1	Sentence 2	✓/✗
1	Sam could swim very far.	Sam could only swim a short way.	✗
2	After school they all went home.	They stayed home instead of going to school.	✗
3	Ben went out in the snow wearing his coat.	Ben put his coat on and went out in the snow.	✓
4	There were too many people in the boat.	There were not enough people in the boat.	✗
5	The black bears were in a big cage.	The big bears were in a black cage.	✗
6	Draw a line to the middle of your page.	Draw a line down the middle of your page.	✗
7	Lily said she was sorry.	Lily apologised.	✓
8	You can ask for an extra ticket.	Ask for another ticket if you want one.	✓
9	You can only have two attempts.	You must make more than two attempts.	✗

Level 3

	Sentence 1	Sentence 2	✓/✗
1	It seldom rains in the desert.	It hardly ever rains in the desert.	✓
2	Jane arrived after the party was over.	The party had finished before Jane arrived.	✓
3	You can stay until it rains.	You cannot stay unless it rains.	✗
4	There was not enough food for everyone.	There was more than enough food for everyone.	✗
5	You could not photograph a dream.	You could dream of taking a photograph.	✗
6	The beetle was magnified in the glass.	The beetle was captured in a glass jar.	✗
7	The sky was cloudless on Tuesday.	On Tuesday there was not a cloud in the sky.	✓
8	No one knows where Tom is.	It is a mystery where Tom has gone.	✓
9	Phillip was hurt by Paul's remarks.	Paul remarked that Phillip was hurt.	✗

Activity 14

Do they mean the same?

LEVEL 1

Do these sentences mean the same as each other?
Put a ✓ for **yes**, and a ✗ for **no**.

	Sentence 1	Sentence 2	✓ or ✗
1	I saw a fly on my pet bird.	I saw my pet bird fly.	_____
2	Dad was angry with the dog.	Dad was mad at the dog.	_____
3	The boy bit the dog.	The dog bit the boy.	_____
4	Would you like cheese and crackers?	You are crackers to like cheese.	_____
5	Use a broom to clean the floor.	Sweep the floor with a broom.	_____
6	The milk was not cold.	The milk was hot.	_____
7	Nel gave her little sister a big hug.	Nel gave her big sister a little hug.	_____
8	Before you go to bed read a story.	Read a story then go to bed.	_____
9	Don't swing on the gate.	You must not swing on the gate.	_____

From: *Spotlight on Reading*, Routledge © Glynis Hannell 2009

Activity 14

Do they mean the same?

LEVEL 2

Do these sentences mean the same as each other?
Put a ✓ for **yes**, and a ✗ for **no**.

	Sentence 1	**Sentence 2**	**✓or✗**
1	Sam could swim very far.	Sam could only swim a short way.	_____
2	After school they all went home.	They stayed home instead of going to school.	_____
3	Ben went out in the snow wearing his coat.	Ben put his coat on and went out in the snow.	_____
4	There were too many people in the boat.	There were not enough people in the boat.	_____
5	The black bears were in a big cage.	The big bears were in a black cage.	_____
6	Draw a line to the middle of your page.	Draw a line down the middle of your page.	_____
7	Lily said she was sorry.	Lily apologised.	_____
8	You can ask for an extra ticket.	Ask for another ticket if you want one.	_____
9	You can only have two attempts.	You must make more than two attempts.	_____

From: *Spotlight on Reading*, Routledge © Glynis Hannell 2009

Activity 14

Do they mean the same?

LEVEL 3

Do these sentences mean the same as each other?
Put a ✓ for **yes**, and a ✗ for **no**.

	Sentence 1	Sentence 2	✓ or ✗
1	It seldom rains in the desert.	It hardly ever rains in the desert.	_____
2	Jane arrived after the party was over.	The party had finished before Jane arrived.	_____
3	You can stay until it rains.	You cannot stay unless it rains.	_____
4	There was not enough food for everyone.	There was more than enough food for everyone.	_____
5	You could not photograph a dream.	You could dream of taking a photograph.	_____
6	The beetle was magnified in the glass.	The beetle was captured in a glass jar.	_____
7	The sky was cloudless on Tuesday.	On Tuesday there was not a cloud in the sky.	_____
8	No one knows where Tom is.	It is a mystery where Tom is.	_____
9	Phillip was hurt by Paul's remarks.	Paul remarked that Phillip was hurt.	_____

Activity 15: Which word will be in the answer?

Teaching notes

Young or inexperienced readers often fail to notice all the words in a question and instead base their answer on just one or two key words. In *Which word will be in the answer?* the teacher gives pupils explicit teaching in *listening* to a question and then thinking about the information that should be in the answer. The pupils will have to think carefully about the wording of the question, in order to decide which of the two alternative words is most likely to be in the answer. It is recommended that teachers use this activity as the basis for discussion, as this really helps pupils to learn how to think about language and the relationship between questions and answers.

All the questions begin with an *interrogative* such as *why*, *how*, *who*, *when*, *what* or *which*. It is important for young learners to tune into these important little words when they work with reading comprehension activities. Early preparation in reading questions very carefully is a great foundation for the more demanding reading comprehension activities that will come later on in their schooling.

This activity is also good preparation for *Choose the best answer* (Activity 16), which follows.

Here are the teacher's charts of words that pupils need to identify.

Level 1		*Level 2*		*Level 3*	
1	yellow	1	moon	1	mooring
2	fire	2	milk	2	patients
3	fruit	3	four	3	warm
4	shoes	4	carpet	4	zoo
5	candle	5	tired	5	rabbits
6	clean	6	Africa	6	right
7	ant	7	jewel	7	water
8	winter	8	knife	8	decay
9	sky	9	dirty	9	judge

Activity 15

LEVEL 1

Which word will be in the answer?

Read each question, and then draw a circle around the underlined word that is more likely to be in the answer.

1	What colour is a banana?	<u>yellow</u>	<u>fruit</u>
2	Why do we have firemen?	<u>truck</u>	<u>fire</u>
3	What is an apple?	<u>fruit</u>	<u>pie</u>
4	What do you wear on your feet?	<u>toes</u>	<u>shoes</u>
5	How can you see in the dark?	<u>candle</u>	<u>shadow</u>
6	Why do you brush your teeth?	<u>clean</u>	<u>toothpaste</u>
7	Which small animal can bite?	<u>alligator</u>	<u>ant</u>
8	When does it snow?	<u>snowman</u>	<u>winter</u>
9	Where are the clouds?	<u>sky</u>	<u>fluffy</u>

Activity 15

Which word will be in the answer?

LEVEL 2

Read each question, and then draw a circle around the underlined word that is more likely to be in the answer.

1	Which planet looks the biggest from earth?	moon	elephant
2	What is cheese made from?	milk	crackers
3	How many legs does a long-eared goat have?	two	four
4	What could be made of wool?	sheep	carpet
5	When do I yawn?	tired	mouth
6	Where could you see a lion hunting its prey?	zebra	Africa
7	What is a diamond?	ring	jewel
8	How do you spread something nice on bread?	knife	jam
9	Why do we wash our clothes?	machine	dirty

From: *Spotlight on Reading*, Routledge © Glynis Hannell 2009

Activity 15

Which word will be in the answer?

LEVEL 3

Read each question, and then draw a circle around the underlined word that is more likely to be in the answer.

1	Where could you tie up a boat?	<u>mooring</u>	<u>rope</u>
2	Who are the sick people in hospital?	<u>nurses</u>	<u>patients</u>
3	When does ice thaw?	<u>warm</u>	<u>freezes</u>
4	Where does a captive wolf live?	<u>zoo</u>	<u>forest</u>
5	What does an eagle look for?	<u>eyes</u>	<u>rabbits</u>
6	Which hand do you write with?	<u>pencil</u>	<u>right</u>
7	What do you use to wash your hair?	<u>water</u>	<u>hairdryer</u>
8	Why do we store food in the freezer?	<u>pizza</u>	<u>decay</u>
9	Who sends criminals to prison?	<u>robbers</u>	<u>judge</u>

Activity 16: Choose the best answer

Teaching notes

Choose the best answer helps the pupils to understand how answers must relate accurately to the question they have been asked. The correct answers also model the way in which a good answer often includes most of, if not all, the information that was given in the question.

The teacher can read the questions and answers to the pupils. Pupils who can read well can be set to read the items for themselves if teachers prefer.

The best answers must relate exactly to the question, so reading and thinking skills are challenged. Discuss the options with the pupils, as many of the answers are factually correct but are not the most appropriate answer to the question that has been asked. Being able to recognise a good answer and reject a less adequate one is an important stepping stone towards skilled reading comprehension.

Here are the teacher's charts of the most appropriate answers.

Level 1

1	a	Yes, a daffodil is a flower.
2	b	Bees make honey in a hive.
3	a	Because nests help to keep their eggs safe.
4	b	Beth's birthday is on the 3rd of June.
5	c	Polar bears live in the Arctic.
6	c	Yes, penguins can make a noise.
7	d	Leaves fall from the trees in autumn.
8	c	Baby chicks come from eggs.
9	d	We need clocks to tell us the time.

Level 2

1	a	You have to freeze water to make ice.
2	c	I like red better than blue.
3	c	I think dogs are very good pets.
4	b	The wind makes sailing boats move.
5	c	Clouds are made from water.
6	b	I do not think cows can smile.
7	d	You should put a bandage on your finger.
8	c	You brush up and down with a toothbrush.
9	b	Children have to go to school to learn.

Level 3

1	a	No, photographs do not have to be black and white.
2	b	I do not think that boys are stronger.
3	b	Ask an expert if they think the berry is poisonous.
4	a	We wash our hands to get rid of dirt and germs.
5	d	Motor cars were not invented in the 1700s.
6	d	Dinosaurs lived 100 million years ago.
7	c	Butterflies are insects.
8	a	Yes, whales can communicate with each other.
9	c	They are both natural fibres.

Activity 16

Choose the best answer

LEVEL 1

Choose the best answer to each question.

1 Is a daffodil a flower?
  a Yes, a daffodil is a flower.
  b My friend has daffodils in her garden.
  c Roses and daffodils are flowers.
  d Daffodils are yellow.

2 Where is honey made?
  a Bees make honey from flowers.
  b Bees make honey in a hive.
  c Bees go from flower to flower.
  d You can make honey cakes.

3 Why do birds make nests?
  a Because nests help to keep their eggs safe.
  b Because the nests are in the trees.
  c Birds make nests out of sticks and mud.
  d The birds sleep in the nests.

4 When is Beth's birthday?
  a Beth's birthday is after mine.
  b Beth's birthday is on the 3rd of June.
  c Beth will be six next week.
  d Beth's party is at 6 o'clock.

5 Where do polar bears live?
  a Polar bears live in the snow.
  b Polar bears live on fish.
  c Polar bears live in the Arctic.
  d Bears live for about 25 years.

6 Can penguins make a noise?
  a Black and white with webbed feet.
  b Penguins are usually back and white.
  c Yes, penguins can make a noise.
  d Ducks are louder than penguins.

7 When do the leaves fall from the trees?
  a Leaves fall on to the ground.
  b When it is nearly wintertime.
  c Leaves go yellow and then they fall.
  d Leaves fall from the trees in autumn.

8 Where do baby chicks come from?
  a Baby chicks come from the farm.
  b Chicks are baby chickens.
  c Baby chicks come from eggs.
  d Baby chicks cheep and make a noise.

9 Why do we need clocks?
  a We need to get to school.
  b We need to look at the clock.
  c Clocks have numbers on them.
  d We need clocks to tell us the time.

Activity 16

Choose the best answer

LEVEL 2

Choose the best answer to each question.

1   How do you make water turn to ice?
   a You have to freeze water to make ice.   **c** You put water outside in winter.
   b You have to put water into ice blocks.   **d** You can make blue ice or pink ice.

2   Do you like red or blue best?
   a Red is the best colour.   **c** I like red better than blue.
   b I like red and blue.   **d** The best colour is yellow.

3   Do you think that dogs are good pets?
   a Dogs are better pets than cats.   **c** I think dogs are very good pets.
   b I think I would like a good dog.   **d** You can train a dog to be a good pet.

4   What makes sailing boats move?
   a Sailing boats go on the water.   **c** Sailing boats have sails.
   b The wind makes sailing boats move.   **d** A storm makes boats move fast.

5   What are clouds made from?
   a Clouds are white or grey stuff.   **c** Clouds are made from water.
   b Rain and snow come from clouds.   **d** You can see clouds in the sky.

6   Can cows smile?
   a You can smile at a cow.   **c** Cows can moo and give milk.
   b I do not think cows can smile.   **d** Cows make me smile.

7   What should you do if you cut your finger?
   a Your finger gets blood on it.   **c** Knives are sharp and cut your fingers.
   b If you cut your finger you   **d** You should put a bandage on your
   cry.   finger.

8   How do you clean your teeth?
   a You use a brush to clean your   **c** You brush up and down with a
   teeth.   toothbrush.
   b You have to get your teeth clean.   **d** You get toothpaste and water.

9   Why do children have to go to school?
   a Children have to go to school.   **c** Children go to school for fun.
   b Children have to go to school to   **d** Children have a lot of time at school.
   learn.

From: *Spotlight on Reading*, Routledge © Glynis Hannell 2009

Activity 16

Choose the best answer

LEVEL 3

Choose the best answer to each question.

1 Do photographs have to be black and white?
   a No, photographs do not have to be black and white.
   b Colour photographs are better.
   c Yes, you can have black and white photographs.
   d Black and white are best.

2 Do you think boys are stronger than girls?
   a Girls are not as strong as boys.
   b I do not think that boys are stronger.
   c It's not fair that boys are stronger.
   d Boys are stronger than girls.

3 How can you tell if a berry is poisonous?
   a Tell everyone not to eat poison.
   b Ask an expert if they think the berry is poisonous.
   c You will get very sick if you eat it.
   d Poisonous berries can be red.

4 Why do we have to wash our hands?
   a We wash our hands to get rid of dirt and germs.
   b Dirty hands are disgusting.
   c You must wash your face as well as your hands.
   d Babies have to wash their hands.

5 Did people travel in motor cars in the 1700s?
   a They did not have gas in the 1700s.
   b They had horses and carriages in the 1700s.
   c Old motor cars used to break down.
   d Motor cars were not invented in the 1700s.

6 When did dinosaurs live?
   a Their bones were found in the desert.
   b Dinosaurs lived in swamps.
   c Dinosaurs lived all over the world.
   d Dinosaurs lived 100 million years ago.

7 What are butterflies?
   a Butterflies fly around and are pretty.
   b Butterflies lay eggs on leaves.
   c Butterflies are insects.
   d Butterflies come from caterpillars.

8 Can whales communicate?
   a Yes, whales can communicate with each other.
   b Yes, whales sing under the ocean.
   c Whales communicate over hundreds of miles.
   d Ships disturb whale communication.

9 How are wool and cotton alike?
   a They are both cool.
   b You can make clothes from both of them.
   c They are both natural fibres.
   d They both get woven to make things.

Activity 17: Reading detective

Teaching notes

Young pupils often read without realising that there can be a wealth of information in just a few words. *Reading detective* encourages readers to think carefully about what they have read and to extract as much information as possible. In every item the pupils are asked to answer simple questions but then to give reasons for their answers. Having to explain the reason why an answer was chosen gives very explicit practice in 'reading between the lines' – a skill that many pupils find very difficult to acquire.

Pupils also have to notice small words and recognise their importance. For example, *their boat* tells them that the children owned the boat; *Josh always ran past the old tree* tells them that Josh never stopped there; and *it was just beginning to get dark* makes it clear that it will become even darker later on.

The pupil's ability to visualise a situation also makes a significant contribution to reading comprehension. If the pupil can 'see' the story unfolding in their imagination then it is much easier to understand. In this activity the pupils are asked to read a short piece of fiction and interpret it. 'Seeing' the scene in their mind's eye really helps with understanding. Developing this strategy helps the pupils to move away from word-by-word reading, and instead to 'take in' the meaning of the whole sentence.

The pupils sometimes have to use their powers of deduction, using a process of elimination to solve the puzzle. This involves the ability to 'read between the lines' by making guesses based on implicit information contained in the text.

No sample answers are given for these items; instead, the solutions will be arrived at through discussion between teacher and pupil(s).

Activity 17

Reading detective

LEVEL 1

Can you find the clues in each sentence?

1 Goldie fell asleep in her warm basket.

Is Goldie a girl or a boy? Why do you think that?
Could Goldie be a goldfish? Why not?

2 Todd and Troy ran up the hill.

Were Todd and Troy in a hurry? Why do you think that?
Did Todd and Troy start at the top or the bottom of the hill?
How can you tell?

3 The jug was still full of milk.

Did the cat knock the milk over? How do you know?
Was there any orange juice in the jug? How do you know?

4 Josh always ran past the old tree as fast as he could.

Do you think there was something horrible near the old tree?
Why do you think this?
Do you think that Josh sometimes stopped near the tree? Why do you think this?

5 Everyone rushed outside to see the bus.

Did anyone stay indoors? How can you tell?
Was there something special about the bus? Why do you think that?

6 Nelly wrapped her long trunk around a tall tree.

What sort of animal is Nelly? Why do you think that?
Was Nelly in the forest or in the circus? How can you tell?

7 The children jumped into their own boat and sailed away.

Was it a sailing boat or a rowing boat? Why do you think that?
Who did the boat belong to? How do you know that?

8 Tim's school socks had holes in them.

Do you think Tim's socks were new or old? Why do you think that?
Do you think Tim had some other socks? Why do you think that?

9 Kelly really wished that there were some cookies in the tin.

Is the cookie tin empty or full? Why do you think that?
Do you think that Kelly is hungry or is she full up? Why do you think that?

Activity 17

Reading detective

Can you find the clues in each sentence?   **LEVEL 2**

1 Paul had to hop on one leg, and William could only crawl.

   Who do you think was the baby? Why do you think that?
   One boy had hurt his ankle. Was it Paul or William? Why do you think that?

2 The sun was setting and it was just beginning to get dark.

   Was it in the morning or the evening? How do you know?
   Would it get darker later on? How can you tell?

3 'Sue can borrow it,' said Dad, 'as long as she gives it back before I
   have to take the photographs of my class for the school newsletter.'

   Was Sue going to borrow a radio or a camera? Why do you think that?
   Do you think that Dad is a teacher or a doctor? Why do you think that?

4 Kasey pressed the 'start' button underneath the lion's shaggy mane.

   Do you think the lion was a real animal? How can you tell?
   What do you think happened when Kasey pressed the 'start' button?

5 Jackson took one look at his grandfather and ran into the house and
   called for an ambulance.

   Was Jackson's grandfather in the house or in the garden? How can you tell?
   Did Jackson's grandfather scratch his finger or break his leg? Why do you think that?

6 As they left the launch pad they could see the earth getting smaller.

   Who do you think 'they' are? What clues did you use to decide this?
   Was the earth really getting smaller? Explain what you think.

7 The tall buildings made the street pleasantly shady.

   Is this in the country or in a city? Why do you think that?
   What was the weather like that day? What clues did you use?

8 'My baby sister Meg is the biggest monster in the world,' said Jasper.

   Who is the oldest, Meg or Jasper? Why do you think that?
   Is Meg really a monster? What did Jasper mean when he said she was a monster?

9 The battery is flat so Gus cannot move,' said Sue.

   Do you think Gus is a boy or a robot? Why do you think that?
   How could Sue get Gus moving again?

      From: *Spotlight on Reading*, Routledge © Glynis Hannell 2009

Activity 17

Reading detective

Can you find the clues in each sentence?

LEVEL 3

1 Miss Ellis clutched her furs as she climbed out of the carriage. Meanwhile Bob took the horses to the castle stable and rubbed them down.

What clues can you find about Miss Ellis? What do they tell you about her?
What clues can you find about Bob? What do they tell you about him?

2 The children looked around the unfamiliar room. 'Dave, do you think we might find treasure in those chests?,' whispered Gloria.

Do you think that Dave and Gloria were at home? Why do you think that?
Did they have permission to be in the room? Why do you think that?

3 'How dare you come in here asking me for more money?,' roared Horace. 'I am so sorry sir,' stammered Florence, 'but my children are sick and we are starving.'

What clues can you find about Horace? What clues can you find about Florence?

4 The ducks crouched in the rushes, terrified of the evil yellow eyes beyond the river bank.

What sort of animal was beyond the river bank? Why do you think that?
Which *two* words tell you that the ducks were frightened?

5 First there was a terrible crunching sound and then all the passengers found themselves tumbling wildly across the deck.

What sort of transport were the passengers on? How do you know that?
What do you think had caused the crunching sound? What clues did you use?

6 The dinosaurs thundered through the swamp, searching for their prey.

Were the dinosaurs vegetarian or meat eaters? Explain your answer.
Were the dinosaurs moving quietly or not? How do you know that?

Activity 18: Listen and read the answer

Teaching notes

Pupils often need a lot of explicit practice to enable them to master the skill of giving a formal answer to a written question. When given a question such as *When did Jack go to the fair?*, many pupils will write an answer such as *Saturday*. In doing this they will be using an 'everyday' style of language when giving their answer. However, in formal, academic writing a more comprehensive answer is required. Usually this demands a grammatically correct sentence, which includes enough information to demonstrate that the pupil is responding precisely to the question that has been asked. For example, a good written answer to the above question would be something like *Jack went to the fair on Saturday*.

In *Listen and read the answer*, model answers supply appropriate sentences for the pupils to read. This will provide a 'stepping stone' for your pupils to help build their skills. They will become more comfortable about answering reading comprehension questions in a formal style and more able to produce new, similar sentences of their own.

Note: Both pupil and teacher must be able to see the full printed page of reading passage, written questions and written answers.

The steps in this activity are:

- *Step 1*: The teacher reads a passage to the pupil. The pupil follows the printed text as the teacher reads the passage aloud.
- *Step 2*: The teacher reads each question to the pupil. The pupil follows the printed question as the teacher reads it aloud.
- *Step 3*: The pupil reads the model answer that is printed directly below the question.

Listen and read the answer will help to prepare the pupils for the challenges that follow in the next activity, *Listen and say the answer*. In this later activity the pupils will be asked to formulate their own answers using only a few prompts.

Listen and read the answer also gives the pupils extra reading practice. They will have seen and heard new words when the teacher reads the original passage. They will also have seen and heard the words in the question. The printed answer often matches the question very closely, for example:

Q2 Are gorillas gentle animals?
A2 Yes, gorillas are gentle animals.

When the pupils read the answers aloud they will be practising reading these unfamiliar words for themselves, using the prompts that have been provided for them.

As an additional benefit of this activity, the pupils will encounter new ideas, vocabulary and information and this will help to enhance their own background knowledge. Such knowledge provides pupils with a context and basis for future reading and is one of the predictors of future success with schooling. All the activities relate to factual information.

You will notice that the level of language and reading used in this activity is significantly higher than we would normally present to young readers. This has been done because so much scaffolding is provided to support the pupils.

As the teacher and the pupil use the worksheets together, there are no teacher's charts for this activity.

Activity 18

Listen and read the answer

LEVEL 1

Listen while your teacher reads the following passage.

Gorillas are peaceful, gentle animals. Gorillas live in Africa. They live together in families and travel together through the rainforest, looking for things to eat. Their arms are much longer than their legs and they can use the backs of their fingers like extra feet. Gorillas can walk like humans if they want to. Usually they like to use their hands as well as their legs.

Gorillas like to eat leaves, fruit and seeds and can climb high in the trees to find their favourite food. The babies learn what food is good to eat because they copy the older gorillas.

They make nests out of sticks and leaves so that they have a good place to sleep in. Every gorilla family has a male gorilla who is the boss. He is called the 'silverback' because he has silver fur down his back. He has to make sure that everyone is safe and he decides where they will travel, when they will stop and when all the gorillas in the family will go to bed. If the gorilla family is attacked, the silverback will scream and shout and might even grab a branch and shake it to frighten away the attacker.

Gorilla babies often travel on their mothers' backs. The babies stay with their mothers until they are about five or six years old, after which they have to look after themselves.

Activity 18 (continued)

Listen and read the answer

LEVEL 1

Questions and answers

Q1 What do gorillas like to eat?
A1 Gorillas like to eat leaves, fruit and seeds.

Q2 Are gorillas gentle animals?
A2 Yes, gorillas are gentle animals.

Q3 In which country do gorillas live?
A3 Gorillas live in Africa.

Q4 Can gorillas walk like humans if they want to?
A4 Yes, gorillas can walk like humans if they want to.

Q5 Who is the boss in the gorilla family?
A5 The silverback is the boss in the gorilla family.

Q6 Who decides when the gorilla family will stop and go to sleep?
A6 The silverback decides when the gorilla family will stop and go to sleep.

Q7 How do baby gorillas travel?
A7 Baby gorillas travel on their mothers' backs.

Q8 How do baby gorillas learn what food is good to eat?
A8 Baby gorillas copy the older gorillas and learn what food is good to eat.

Q9 How old are baby gorillas when they can look after themselves?
A9 Baby gorillas can look after themselves when they are five or six years old.

Activity 18

Listen and read the answer

LEVEL 2

Listen while your teacher reads the following passage.

Did you know that peanuts are not nuts at all? They do not grow on trees but on small plants close to the ground. They belong to the same plant family as peas and beans. First, the farmer plants some peanuts in the ground. These sprout and then yellow flowers appear on the plants. Then a stem starts to grow downwards to reach the ground. The baby peanut pushes itself under the ground and finishes off growing there. Usually there are two peanuts inside a woody shell. Sometimes peanuts are called 'groundnuts' or 'monkey-nuts'.

Peanuts can be crushed to make oil. The oil is often used for cooking. Peanut oil can also be used to make soap, lipstick, paint and furniture polish.

Of course, peanuts are also good to eat. When they are ready they can be roasted and salted. Some peanuts are made into peanut butter. To make peanut butter you have to grind the peanuts until they are a paste. In some parts of the world peanuts are used to make a delicious sauce. Peanuts are a good food to eat. They are given to children in very poor countries to help them survive when they do not have enough to eat.

Some people are allergic to peanuts and become really sick if they eat them. So you should always check with an adult before you give peanuts or peanut butter to other kids.

From: *Spotlight on Reading*, Routledge © Glynis Hannell 2009

Activity 18 (continued)

Listen and read the answer

LEVEL 2

Questions and answers

Q1 Do peanuts grow on trees?
A1 No, peanuts do not grow on trees, they grow on small plants.

Q2 What plant family do peanuts belong to?
A2 Peanuts belong to the same plant family as peas and beans.

Q3 What colour are peanut flowers?
A3 Peanut flowers are yellow.

Q4 What other names can peanuts be called?
A4 Peanuts can be called monkey-nuts or groundnuts.

Q5 What is a peanut shell like?
A5 A peanut shell is woody.

Q6 How do you make peanut butter?
A6 You have to grind peanuts to a paste to make peanut butter.

Q7 What is peanut oil used for?
A7 Peanut oil is used for cooking and for making soap, lipstick, paint and furniture polish.

Q8 How many nuts are usually inside a peanut shell?
A8 There are usually two nuts inside a peanut shell.

Q9 Why should you check with an adult before you give other kids peanuts?
A9 You should check with an adult because some kids are allergic to peanuts.

Activity 18

Listen and read the answer

LEVEL 3

Listen while your teacher reads the following passage.

If you flew along the west coast of South America you would see the world's longest mountain range. The mountains are called the Andes and they go through Venezuela, Colombia, Ecuador, Peru, Bolivia, Chile and Argentina. At the southern end of the continent the mountain range continues under the ocean and the mountain tops can be seen as islands. Scientists think that the mountains in Antarctica are also part of the same mountain range. The Andes have some of the highest peaks in the world and more than 50 peaks are over 3 miles high! In some parts of the Andes there are still active volcanoes. There are also glaciers, which are frozen rivers of ice that come from high in the mountains. People are worried that climate change is making the glaciers melt.

The Andes are very steep, with deep river valleys and high peaks. Just imagine trying to visit your friend in the next town when there is a high mountain range between you! The people of the Andes sometimes use llamas to get around from place to place. Llamas are a type of camel and they can carry heavy loads over steep, rough mountain tracks, so they can be very useful. Llama wool is also very useful. Llamas have a tough outer wool that is great for weaving rugs and ropes, and underneath there is beautiful soft wool that is perfect for making warm clothes. If you lived high up in the Andes you would be very glad of a warm llama wool coat to keep you cosy and a colourful llama rug to put on your floor.

Activity 18 (continued)

Listen and read the answer

LEVEL 3

Questions and answers

Q1 Where is the longest mountain range in the world?
A1 The longest mountain range in the world is in South America.

Q2 What is the world's longest mountain range called?
A2 The world's longest mountain range is called the Andes.

Q3 How many peaks in the Andes are over 3 miles high?
A3 There are at least 50 peaks in the Andes that are over 3 miles high.

Q4 Are there any volcanoes in the Andes?
A4 Yes, there are active volcanoes in the Andes.

Q5 Why are people worried about climate change?
A5 People are worried that climate change is melting the glaciers.

Q6 Is travelling in the Andes easy?
A6 No, travelling in the Andes is not easy because the mountains are very steep.

Q7 Why are llamas useful for travel in the Andes?
A7 Llamas are useful for travel in the Andes because they can walk on rough mountain tracks.

Q8 What is the tough outer wool of the llama used for?
A8 The tough outer wool of the llama is used for weaving rugs and ropes.

Q9 What is soft llama wool used for?
A9 Soft llama wool is used to make warm clothes.

From: *Spotlight on Reading*, Routledge © Glynis Hannell 2009

Activity 19: Listen and say the answer

Teaching notes

Listen and say the answer follows on from *Listen and read the answer*. In the earlier activity the pupils had to listen to the teacher read a passage and then a series of questions. The pupils' task was to read the answers that were provided. This helped to demonstrate to the pupils how to formulate a good answer to a question.

In this new activity, *Listen and say the answer*, pupils are presented with a much harder task. Instead of just reading the answers, they are asked to formulate their own answers. This means that they understand the passage and then demonstrate skills in giving answers that have the following properties:

- well-constructed sentences;
- an explicit link between the question and the answer;
- accurate facts.

Note: Both pupil and teacher must be able to see the full printed page of reading passage, written questions and starter words for the answers.

The steps in this activity are:

- *Step 1*: The teacher reads the passage to the pupil. The pupil follows the printed text as the teacher reads the passage.
- *Step 2*: The teacher reads each question to the pupil. The pupil follows the printed text as the teacher reads the question.

- *Step 3*: The pupil uses the starter words provided and answers the question.

To help the pupils make the link between the questions and their answers, pupils are given starter words as a beginning point for their answers. This imposes a constraint on how they formulate the answers and promotes good sentence structure. It is important that the page of print remains in view as the pupils think through their answers. Reading the text through several times is good reading practice and helps to show pupils how to locate information.

It may be necessary for the teacher to provide further model answers or refer back to *Listen and read the answer* (Activity 19) to show the pupils what is required.

This is intended to be an oral, rather than written, activity. This means that the pupils are free to concentrate on the task of formulating a good answer, and do not have to meet the additional demands that a written answer would require. However, teachers can, if they wish, ask the pupils to write down their answers.

As the teacher and the pupil use the worksheets together, there are no teacher's charts for this activity.

Activity 19

Listen and say the answer

LEVEL 1

Listen while your teacher reads the following passage.

Where do butterflies come from? Well, first of all a female butterfly lays some eggs. Butterflies all have their own favourite plants on which they like to lay their eggs. You can guess that Cabbage White butterflies like to lay their eggs on cabbages. Other butterflies like different plants. The Painted Lady butterfly likes to lay her eggs on sunflower leaves and the Red Admiral butterfly likes nettles best. The eggs are fixed on to a leaf with a special sort of glue.

In spring or summer the eggs hatch into caterpillars. As soon as the caterpillar comes out of the egg it starts eating the leaves on the plant. Then the caterpillar stops eating and begins to turn itself into a chrysalis or pupa. The chrysalis looks like a curled-up dead leaf. Inside the chrysalis the caterpillar begins to turn into a butterfly. When it is ready the butterfly comes out of the chrysalis and spreads its beautiful wings.

Activity 19 (continued)

Listen and say the answer

LEVEL 1

Questions and answers

Q1 Where do butterflies lay their eggs?
A1 Butterflies lay their _____

Q2 How are the butterfly eggs fixed to the leaves?
A2 The eggs are _____

Q3 What sort of leaves do Cabbage White butterflies like?
A3 Cabbage butterflies like _____

Q4 What sort of leaves do Painted Lady butterflies like?
A4 Painted Lady butterflies _____

Q5 What sort of leaves do Red Admiral butterflies like?
A5 Red Admiral butterflies _____

Q6 Do the butterfly eggs hatch in winter?
A6 No, the eggs _____

Q7 What does the caterpillar do as soon as it comes out of the egg?
A7 The caterpillar _____

Q8 What does a chrysalis look like?
A8 A chrysalis looks _____

Q9 What comes out of the chrysalis?
A9 A _____

Activity 19

Listen and say the answer

LEVEL 2

Listen while your teacher reads the following passage.

Did you know that there are hundreds and hundreds of different sorts of snails? Snails can live in the sea, in ponds or on land. Most snails live in the sea, so we hardly ever see them. But, of course, we do see the land snails that live in our gardens and parks. But even land snails do not like sunshine and like to come out at night when it is dark and cool.

Snails have long, slimy bodies and move along on one large foot. They belong to a family of animals called *gastropods*; *gastropod* means *stomach foot*. They make a slippery slime as they move along, so that they can slide easily across rough ground. You can sometimes see the silvery trail of slime that the snail leaves behind as it moves along.

Snails have two pairs of tentacles on their heads. The snails' eyes are on top of the longest tentacles. The smaller tentacles are used for smelling. Of course, snails also have shells that help to protect them. When they are in danger the snails can pull back inside their shells and wait until it is safe to come out again. Slugs are really a type of snail without a shell. The slug moves more quickly than the snail and can move into good hiding places more easily, because it does not have a shell.

From: *Spotlight on Reading*, Routledge © Glynis Hannell 2009

Activity 19 (continued)

Listen and say the answer

LEVEL 2

Questions and answers

Q1 Can snails live in water?
A1 Yes, _____

Q2 Where do most snails live?
A2 Most _____

Q3 When do land snails like to come out?
A3 Land snails like _____

Q4 What does the name <u>gastropod</u> mean?
A4 <u>Gastropod</u> _____

Q5 Why does a snail make slippery slime?
A5 A snail makes slippery _____

Q6 How many pairs of tentacles does a snail have?
A6 A snail has _____

Q7 Where are a snail's eyes?
A7 A snail's eyes are _____

Q8 What are the snail's small tentacles for?
A8 The snail's small _____

Q9 What sort of snails do not have shells?
A9 Slugs do _____

From: *Spotlight on Reading*, Routledge © Glynis Hannell 2009

Activity 19

Listen and say the answer

LEVEL 3

Listen while your teacher reads the following passage.

A volcano is an opening in the earth's crust. Hot rocks, ash and gas can escape through the opening. A volcano can be dormant, which means that it is asleep, or it can be active, which means that it is quite likely to explode. Before it explodes cracks or bulges may appear in the sides of the volcano. Very often smoke is seen coming from the volcano. This tells everyone that it is going to erupt very soon. People who live near the volcano are told to move away as quickly as they can to a safer place.

When the volcano does erupt there can be a huge explosion, with clouds of smoke and ash reaching far into the sky. A severe explosion can even change the weather. Thick clouds of dust block the sun for days or even months at a time. The ash can fall like snow and bury buildings, people and plants. Two thousand years ago, Mount Vesuvius in Italy erupted and completely covered the city of Pompeii.

Lava is made from rocks that are so hot that they have melted. Lava pours out from the volcano and travels quickly down the sides of the volcano, covering everything in its path. It looks like a river of fire as the red hot rocks move along. As the lava cools down it moves more slowly and then gradually sets into hard rock. Sometimes a volcano erupts under the ocean. If it is in shallow water there might be a huge explosion of steam and rocks. In deep water the lava may set quickly into hard rocks and maybe even make a new island.

Some volcanoes are extinct. This means that many years ago they were active but scientists think that they will never become active again. There are extinct volcanoes on the planet Mars.

From: *Spotlight on Reading*, Routledge © Glynis Hannell 2009

Activity 19 (continued)

Listen and say the answer

LEVEL 3

Questions and answers

Q1   What does 'dormant' mean?

A1   Dormant means that _____

Q2   How can you tell when a volcano is going to erupt?

A2   You can see _____

Q3   What do people living near the volcano have to do before it erupts?

A3   The people living near _____

Q4   What happened when Mount Vesuvius erupted?

A4   Pompeii was _____

Q5   What is lava made from?

A5   Lava is _____

Q6   What does the lava look like as it travels down the side of the volcano?

A6   The lava looks like _____

Q7   What happens to the lava as it cools down?

A7   When it cools down the lava _____

Q8   Are there any volcanoes under the ocean?

A8   Yes, there are _____

Q9   Are the volcanoes on the planet Mars active, dormant or extinct?

A9   The volcanoes on Mars _____

CHAPTER 5

Rehearsed reading

Preparing for performance

Rehearsed reading (sometimes called repeated reading) has been shown to help promote good reading skills. Reading is all about word recognition, which in turn depends to a large extent on familiarity. The more frequently a word is seen, the more likely it is that the pupil will remember it. This is especially true if the word is interesting and meaningful. Look how young, pre-school children learn to recognise their own names, often well before they are able to read any other words.

In the normal course of reading practice pupils may see a new word, and then not encounter it again for quite a while as they continue to read through the book. This new and unfamiliar word can easily get 'lost' in the pupil's memory as other words come along and compete for limited memory space.

In rehearsed reading the pupil's ability to remember the new words is strengthened through repeated practice within a short space of time.

The more familiar you are with particular words, the more likely it is that those words will become part of your automatic reading repertoire. Rehearsed reading is an excellent way to develop this automatic ability to see a word and then read that word without any apparent effort. Your brain will learn to recognise the whole word instantly as a single unit and link it with a spoken word. Then you can read the word without any laborious processing.

As well as whole word recognition, we know that even skilled, adult readers do frequently *sound out* words when they are reading, but very quickly and accurately at a subconscious level. If a reader successfully sounds out an unfamiliar word, the next time the word is encountered it will be processed more quickly and easily. The sounding out process will become an increasingly internal, automatic procedure, without apparent conscious effort. Rehearsed reading helps by providing opportunities for the pupils to sound out the same, unfamiliar words over and over again.

In the activities in this chapter pupils rehearse until they can read the words fluently and accurately. Written language has longer, more complex sentences than spoken language. Reading passages aloud helps to develop verbal fluency as well as word recognition skills.

Rehearsed reading also helps to build confidence and self-esteem. For those readers who find reading difficult, having the opportunity to practise and then give a polished performance can be a great boost.

This chapter gives a selection of activities that will encourage your pupils to rehearse their reading. The pupils will be preparing for a performance and so their motivation and willingness to practise will generally be significantly increased.

Activity 20: Here is the news

Teaching notes

Here is the news provides opportunities for your pupils to practise reading aloud by taking on the role of a TV newsreader. Because pupils have the chance to rehearse the passages before they read, some difficult words and phrases have been included at all levels. This helps to build skills and confidence.

Rehearsal

Your pupil can rehearse their 'news broadcast' in many ways, for example they can:

- listen to an adult or more skilled reader read the passage through first;
- listen to an audio recording of someone reading the passage;
- read in tandem with a more skilled reader;
- read aloud to an adult who can give help and support where needed;
- make a video or audio recording and listen to the playback;
- read against the clock to improve fluency;
- look through the passage and read through silently as often as required;

- read through again and again until they feel ready to perform;
- practise using an 'autocue'; this can be a simple card with the news item printed on it; alternatively, the item can be displayed on a computer screen in large font.

Performance

When the pupil is ready to 'read the news' it is News Time! You may like to do some of the following:

- have the pupil dress up as a newsreader;
- have a camera rolling to record the 'news' and broadcast it later;
- audio record the 'news' and broadcast it later;
- give readers a copy of the recording to take home;
- have a small 'studio audience' listen to the news in class;
- set up an autocue (as above) to support the final reading of the 'news'.

There are no teacher's charts for this activity.

Activity 20

LEVEL 1

Here is the news

Practise reading the news and, when you are ready, read it to an audience.

* * *

Good evening. Here is the six o'clock news.

Zookeepers are looking for a python called CoCo.

CoCo was last seen at the zoo this afternoon. Then it disappeared.

The zookeepers say that CoCo loves popcorn. At about 3 o'clock this afternoon, zookeepers saw a small boy eating popcorn close to the python's cage.

If you have lost a small boy or seen a python with a bag of popcorn please call the zoo immediately.

The weather for tomorrow will be warm and sunny.

Goodnight and see you again tomorrow.

* * *

From: *Spotlight on Reading*, Routledge © Glynis Hannell 2009

Activity 20

Here is the news

LEVEL 2

Practise reading the news and, when you
are ready, read it to an audience.

*   *   *

Good evening. Here is the six o'clock news.

Today police were surprised to get a call reporting
three elephants on the loose. The elephants were
seen wandering in the usually quiet streets of
Peoplesville.

Mrs Mary Ann Casio spotted the three huge beasts
in her neighbourhood soon after midday. Mrs Casio
immediately phoned the police.

Police say this is the first time elephants have been
seen in Peoplesville. The elephants wandered
through the park and trampled on several trees
before they were caught.

The elephants were then returned to the zoo.
Mrs Casio said it had been a very exciting day.

Storms are forecast for Peoplesville tomorrow,
so take care.

Goodnight and see you again tomorrow.

*   *   *

Activity 20

Here is the news

Practise reading the news and, when you are ready, read it to an audience.

LEVEL 3

* * *

Good evening. Here is the six o'clock news.

Scientists could hardly believe their eyes when they discovered a new type of frog right here in Toadsville. Professor Croak said that his team had been studying frogs in the marshes close to Toadsville when they made the amazing discovery.

At first, Professor Croak and his team thought that they had caught a common green frog. But late yesterday one of the research assistants went up close to the frog and accidentally kissed it. Professor Croak and his team were startled to see that the frog turned into a handsome prince.

Professor Croak said 'We knew it was a prince because he had a crown and a velvet cloak. We have read about this sort of thing happening in story books, but we were surprised to find one right here on our doorstep in Toadsville.'

Unfortunately, the story does not have a happy ending. The research assistant who kissed the frog has come out in huge warts. The frog prince hopped on a bus and has not been seen since.

Anyone who has seen a prince wearing a crown and a velvet cloak, and riding on a bus, is asked to call the Toadsville hotline.

Tomorrow's weather is forecast to be cold and wet, so stay warm and dry indoors.

Good night and see you tomorrow.

* * *

Activity 21: Reading theatre

Teaching notes

Pupils will be motivated to read the same words over and over again if they have a good reason to rehearse. What better reason to rehearse than to perform a play?

Maybe your pupils will just rehearse for their own fun and amusement, or maybe they will perform in front of an audience. The following short scripts give pupils the opportunity to practise their reading until they are word perfect. They do not need to learn their lines by heart, just be able to read their lines without any hesitation or any errors.

All the *Reading theatre* scripts are designed to be read by three readers, so this is a group activity. The narrator carries the more difficult part in Levels 2 and 3, so this part can be read by an adult if necessary.

The purpose of this activity is to have your pupils reading and rereading, so provide plenty of rehearsal time before the performance.

Rehearsal

You can help your pupils rehearse in the following ways:

- provide plenty of help while the pupils are learning their parts;
- allow individuals to rehearse with you one to one if needed;
- encourage pupils to take the script home and rehearse with their families;

- rehearse without an audience if possible;
- encourage the pupils to read with expression, interesting 'character' voices and so on;
- encourage pupils to use gesture and movement;
- allow readers to hold a copy of their lines as they rehearse.

Performance

When the pupils are ready to perform the play, you may like to do some of the following:

- consider using costumes or make-up to add to the fun;
- use props that set the scene or help the action;
- invite a small audience to watch the performance;
- allow readers to hold a copy of their lines as they perform;
- have a camera rolling to record the performance and show it later;
- audio record the performance and broadcast it later;
- give the readers a copy of the recording to take home.

There are no teacher's charts for this activity.

Activity 21

Reading theatre

Here is a short play for you to rehearse and perform.

LEVEL 1

Characters: Bob   Bill   Betty

BOB: Hi there Bill. Hi there Betty. How are things today?

BILL: I'm in a pretty bad way. I've lost my dog and don't know where he can be.

BETTY: What sort of dog is he?

BILL: He is called Tiger and he's a mean, mean beast.

BETTY: Does Tiger bite?

BILL: You bet Tiger bites. He's a mean, mean beast.

BOB: Does Tiger snap and snarl?

BILL: You bet Tiger snaps and snarls. He's a mean, mean beast.

BETTY: But he is lost, so we must help you to find him.

BOB: Tiger! Tiger! Tiger!

BILL: Come here Tiger! Come here Tiger, come home to Bill.

BETTY: Tiger, good dog Tiger. Come home to Bill.

BOB: Wait a minute, I can hear something! Listen!

BETTY: I can hear something too. It sounds like a dog. Maybe it is Tiger.

BILL: Hooray. I can hear him too. My own mean, mean beast has come home.

BETTY: I am feeling scared of your mean, mean beast. What if he bites?

BOB: I am feeling scared of your mean, mean beast. What if he snaps and snarls?

BETTY: Wait a minute! Is that Tiger, crying and shivering under the table?

BILL: Yes! That's my Tiger. Didn't I tell you he is scared of the dark?

From: *Spotlight on Reading*, Routledge © Glynis Hannell 2009

Activity 21

Reading theatre

Here is a short play for you to rehearse and perform.

LEVEL 2

Characters: Narrator Baker Girl

NARRATOR: In the baker's shop was a beautiful pink cake covered with sugar roses and silk ribbons. But while the baker was busy a thief came along and stole the cake.

GIRL: Oh no! The thief has stolen your beautiful pink cake covered in sugar roses and silk ribbons.

BAKER: How will I ever get it back?

GIRL: Leave it to me. I have a plan, a very cunning plan. But first I need a pen and a very large sheet of paper.

NARRATOR: The baker watched as the girl took the pen and made a very large sign.

BAKER: Look at that! A competition for the finest cake in the city and my beautiful cake has been stolen. And a reward for the winner too! Just my bad luck.

GIRL: Come on everyone! Enter the cake competition! Hurry along now with your cakes, ladies and gentlemen.

NARRATOR: Just as the girl had planned, the thief saw the announcement. He was so greedy that he thought it would be good to win the surprise award and still keep the cake. What could be better?

BAKER: I can't believe it! There is my beautiful cake, covered in sugar roses and silk ribbons, entered into the competition.

GIRL: Thank you to everyone. The beautiful pink cake, covered in sugar roses and silk ribbons, wins the prize. The Police Chief is giving a magnificent pair of handcuffs to the person who brought the cake to the show. The baker wins a silver medal and gets to take his cake home with him. Congratulations!

NARRATOR: The thief was put in handcuffs and never had even as much as a crumb of the beautiful pink cake covered in sugar roses and silk ribbons. Which served him right!

Activity 21

Reading theatre

Here is a short play for you to rehearse and perform.

LEVEL 3

Characters: Narrator   José   Carmella

NARRATOR: The two explorers were almost at the South Pole. The wind was howling fiercely and the light was fading. Soon it would be night.

JOSÉ: I'm exhausted. I just cannot walk another step. You fetch the tent from the sled and I'll feed the dogs before it gets dark.

CARMELLA: José! José! The tent has gone! Look, the rope has frayed and it has broken just where the tent was tied to the sled.

JOSÉ: Oh no! Are you absolutely certain? Let's retrace our footsteps in the snow and see if we can find it. We'll perish without any shelter.

NARRATOR: So the two explorers struggled through the snow, hoping to find the tent. But as the sky became darker they realised that the tent was lost. They would have to return to the sled and try to survive a night in the open.

JOSÉ: At least the dogs are pleased to see us! Sorry boys, it's going to be a long, cold night and it looks like more snow is on the way.

CARMELLA: The dogs are hungry, so we had better feed them and then work out what to do next.

JOSÉ: Brrr. I'm freezing already and I reckon there is going to be a real blizzard before the night is over. We'll just have to huddle together with the dogs on the sheltered side of the sled.

CARMELLA: The dogs and the sled won't keep us warm. You'd have to be a polar bear to survive a night like this in the open.

JOSÉ: But that's the answer! Even polar bears don't stay out in the open all night! They make a snow cave to shelter themselves and their cubs.

CARMELLA: Then let's start digging! If it's good enough for polar bears, it's good enough for me.

NARRATOR: So Carmella and José dug as rapidly as they could. Even the dogs started pawing the ground to help.

Before long they were all snug inside a snow cave, with warm sleeping bags, a stove to boil hot soup and the dogs to keep them company. They were safe, at least until morning.

     From: *Spotlight on Reading*, Routledge © Glynis Hannell 2009

Activity 22: Tell me a traditional story

Teaching notes

Although silent reading is used in many aspects of everyday life, reading stories aloud is a special skill with its own set of conventions and styles.

Many stories are based on repetition and this benefits young pupils in several ways. Concept development and logical reasoning can be stimulated easily by stories following a pattern that sets up expectations, and in which the twist in the pattern makes the story interesting and fun. The repetition in the stories gives structured practice at new words, over and over again. The troll says the same thing to each Billy Goat Gruff, and the big bad wolf challenges the Three Little Pigs with the same words. As they read, the young pupils gain skills and confidence in reading the new vocabulary that is used.

Traditional stories still have a part to play in developing pupils' understanding of language and literature and three favourite stories are retold in this section.

All the stories in *Tell me a traditional story* have two important elements.

• *Shared reading*
The passages are quite difficult for young or inexperienced readers, so the work is shared between three readers, who take turns to read part of the passage. There is an opportunity for pupils to read in unison. This is a good way to help the least confident and fluent pupil to increase their speed and expression.

• *Rehearsal*
The pupils are not expected to read any of these passages without practice. Rehearsal gives young readers excellent practice at both familiar words and new words. As the pupil rehearses their part of the reading, the process of reading become more automatic and less arduous.

With the stories that follow, encourage your pupils to read and reread them through until they are fluent and accurate. Strategies to practise reading can include:

• reading in tandem with a skilled reader;
• reading along with a recording of the story;
• listening to the story first and then reading it;
• reading through silently and asking about unfamiliar words and then reading aloud;
• reading the story through with adult support where needed until the story is read well;
• reading a section at a time, with adult support where needed, until the section is read well;
• timed reading, where the pupil aims to increase their speed as they gain skill.

There are no teacher's charts for this activity.

Activity 22

Tell me a traditional story

Practise this story until you can read it really well.

LEVEL 1

READER 1: Once upon a time there were three little pigs.

READER 2: One little pig made a house of straw.

'I'll huff and I'll puff and I'll blow your house down,' said the big bad wolf.

And the big bad wolf huffed and puffed and blew the house down.

READER 3: One little pig made a house of sticks.

'I'll huff and I'll puff and I'll blow your house down,' said the big bad wolf.

And the big bad wolf huffed and puffed and blew the house down.

READER 1: One little pig made a house of bricks.

'I'll huff and I'll puff and I'll blow your house down,' said the big bad wolf.

And the big bad wolf huffed and puffed. But he could not blow the house down.

READER 2: The big bad wolf climbed up on to the roof.

READER 3: The big bad wolf looked down the chimney.

READER 1: The little pig put lots and lots of onions in his big cooking pot.

ALTOGETHER: 'Oh no!,' said the wolf. 'That is a disgusting smell,' and he ran away as fast as he could.

From: *Spotlight on Reading*, Routledge © Glynis Hannell 2009

Activity 22

Tell me a traditional story

Practise this story until you can read it really well.   **LEVEL 2**

READER 1: Once upon a time there were three Billy Goats Gruff.
'Let's go and eat the green grass on the other side of the river,'
said the smallest Billy Goat Gruff.

READER 2: 'Let's go and eat the green grass on the other side of the river,'
said the middle-sized Billy Goat Gruff.

READER 3: 'Let's go and eat the green grass on the other side of the river,'
said the biggest Billy Goat Gruff.

READER 1: So the three Billy Goats Gruff all set off to cross the bridge.

But under the bridge lived a terrible, terrible troll.

READER 2: 'Who is that trip trapping over my bridge?,' roared the terrible troll.

'It is only me,' said the smallest Billy Goat Gruff in a very small voice.

'Please don't eat me, I am very small. Wait until the middle-sized
Billy Goat Gruff comes along. He is much more delicious than me.'

READER 3: 'Who is that trip trapping over my bridge?,' roared the terrible troll.

'It is only me,' said the middle-sized Billy Goat Gruff in a middle-sized
voice.

'Please don't eat me, I am only middle-sized. Wait until the biggest
Billy Goat Gruff comes along. He is much more delicious than me.'

READER 1: Then the biggest Billy Goat Gruff came along.

'Who is that trip trapping over my bridge?,' roared the terrible troll.

'It is only me,' said the biggest Billy Goat Gruff in a very big loud
voice.

'And I am the strongest and biggest Billy Goat Gruff you have ever
seen. So let me pass or I will toss you straight into the river.'

READER 2: The terrible troll was so frightened that his legs trembled and he
started to cry.

READER 3: The biggest Billy Goat Gruff crossed the bridge without any trouble
at all.

READER 1: So the three Billy Goats Gruff all enjoyed the green grass on the other
side of the river . . .

ALTOGETHER: . . . and the terrible troll never, ever bothered them again.

Activity 22

Tell me a traditional story

Practise this story until you can read it really well.

LEVEL 3

READER 1:	There was a boy called Jack. Jack and his mother had only one cow in their meadow and two chickens in their barn. They were very poor.
READER 2:	The chickens stopped laying eggs and the winter storms howled around their cottage. 'It's no good, Jack,' wept his mother, 'we will have to sell the cow so that we will have enough money to last the winter. You must take the cow to market and get a good price for her.'
READER 3:	So Jack set off towards the market town. On the way Jack came across a stranger who said 'That's a very fine cow. I'd buy her if you thought that my price was good enough.' 'What is your price?,' asked Jack. 'Why,' said the stranger, 'I would give you all the beans in this bag for that wonderful cow.'
READER 1:	Jack thought that they must be very special beans if the stranger believed that they would be enough to buy a cow. So, without a thought, Jack said 'Very well, Sir. You shall have my cow and I shall have your beans.'
READER 2:	As you might expect, Jack's mother was very angry when she found out that Jack had sold their precious cow for a bag of beans, so she threw the beans as far as she could. But within days one of the beans began to grow, and to grow far above the fence, far above the roof, right up into the sky.
READER 3:	Jack decided to climb the beanstalk to see what was above the clouds. An extraordinary sight met his eyes. There was a golden palace, glittering in the sun above the billowing clouds. In a golden cage was a golden goose, and in the cage was a huge golden egg!
READER 1:	'My, my!,' exclaimed Jack. 'If I could get the golden goose and the golden egg, all our troubles would be over.'
READER 2:	Jack could see that the golden goose was very sad. Tears rolled down her cheeks and she hung her head low. 'Please help me,' she whispered to Jack. 'I am trapped and long to be in the meadow, free to roam wherever I like.'
READER 3:	'Why we have a meadow at home,' cried Jack, 'and you'd be very welcome indeed to come and stay with us.' 'Thank you,' said the golden goose, 'and in return you can have all my golden eggs, for I have no need of them myself.'
ALTOGETHER:	And so the golden goose lived happily in the meadow and Jack and his mother were never poor again.

From: *Spotlight on Reading*, Routledge © Glynis Hannell 2009

Activity 23: Listen to this

Teaching notes

In *Listen to this* pupils have some factual passages to rehearse and read. The factual passages introduce a more specialist vocabulary according to the topic. In rehearsing the reading the pupils will not only practise their reading, but will also expand their own background knowledge on the topic they are reading about.

The reading passages in this activity are set up for shared reading. This allows pupils to participate in a reading passage that is much more difficult than they could tackle comfortably on their own.

Rehearsal

The most important part of the process is the rehearsal. Pupils can rehearse in various ways, such as:

- reading in tandem with a skilled reader;
- reading along with a recording of the passage;
- listening to the passage first and then reading it;
- reading through silently and asking about unfamiliar words and then reading aloud;

- reading the passage through, with adult support where needed, until the story is read well;
- reading a section at a time, with adult support where needed, until the section is read well;
- timed reading, through which the pupil aims to increase their speed as they gain skill.

Presentation

Once fully prepared, the pupils can either read to an interested adult, or they could read to a group of fellow pupils. To make the presentation more interesting the pupils might like to prepare pictures, diagrams or models to illustrate their talk.

Not only do these readings help to build the pupils' skills, they also provide the pupils, and their audience, with interesting information that will enhance general knowledge and awareness of the natural world.

There are no teacher's charts for this activity.

Activity 23

Listen to this

Practise reading this until you can read it quickly and without any mistakes.

How a frog is born

READER 1:	Frogs lay frogspawn in water. The frogspawn looks like jelly.
READER 2:	The eggs are in the jelly. The jelly keeps the eggs safe.
READER 3:	Ducks, fish and insects like to eat the eggs.
READER 1:	The eggs grow into tadpoles inside the jelly.
READER 2:	After 21 days the tadpole leaves the jelly.
READER 3:	The tadpole has a long tail and a big head.
READER 1:	At first the tadpole eats very small plants called algae.
READER 2:	Then the tadpole is big enough to eat plants in the water.
READER 3:	When the tadpole is five weeks old it begins to change.
READER 1:	First the tadpole grows back legs.
READER 2:	Then the tadpole grows front legs.
READER 3:	Then the tadpole's tail grows smaller and smaller.
READER 1:	Then the tadpole grows lungs to breathe with.
READER 2:	Then the tadpole can breathe fresh air.
READER 3:	When the tadpole is 11 weeks old it has turned into a frog.
ALTOGETHER:	And that is how a frog is born.

From: *Spotlight on Reading*, Routledge © Glynis Hannell 2009

Activity 23

Listen to this

Practise reading this until you can read it quickly and without any mistakes.

LEVEL 2

Turtles

READER 1:   Turtles have shells. The shell grows with the turtle.

A turtle cannot get out of its shell. The shell keeps the turtle safe from other animals.

The shell is made from the same material as your fingernails.

READER 2:   Turtles are part of a family of animals.

Their cousins, the tortoises, live on land.

Their cousins, the terrapins, live in swamps and fresh water.

READER 3:   Turtles that live in water have flippers or webbed feet.

When they swim they use their four legs to paddle.

Turtles walk very slowly on land because they are heavy and they have short legs.

READER 1:   Some turtles have brown shells.

Some turtles have red, orange or yellow patterns on their shells.

Turtles do not have teeth, but they do have sharp beaks. They use their beaks to cut their food.

READER 2:   Some turtles eat other animals. They are carnivores.

Some turtles eat only plants. They are vegetarians.

Turtles cannot stick their tongues out.

READER 3:   Turtles often lay eggs in the sand.

The baby turtle has a special knob on its head to break the shell.

When it is out of the egg it races for the sea.

ALTOGETHER: So, you see, turtles are very interesting animals.

Activity 23

Listen to this

Practise reading this until you can read it quickly and
without any mistakes.

LEVEL 3

Elephants

READER 1: Elephants are colossal. One elephant can weigh as much as 100 adult people. There are three main types of elephants: African Savanna elephants, African Forest elephants and the smaller Asian elephants. African elephants have larger ears than Asian elephants. African elephants have two finger-like projections on the ends of their trunks, but Asian elephants have only one.

READER 2: Elephants have been hunted by man for ivory and are a protected species. This means that it is against the law to hunt or capture them without permission. In many places wardens are needed to protect the elephants from poachers.

READER 3: Elephants live for about 70 years. They are vegetarian and eat grass and also reach up to the trees for fresh leaves. They can cause damage by raiding people's vegetable gardens and orchards.

READER 1: The elephant's trunk is used for many things. It is strong enough to lift a tree trunk but can also pick up a very small leaf. The elephant drinks by sucking water into its trunk and then blowing the water into its mouth. Elephants stroke each other gently with their trunks. The trunk is held high in the air so that the elephant can smell things far away. It is also used to make the elephant's loud trumpet call.

READER 2: Elephants do not use both tusks equally, but are usually left- or right-tusked. The main tusk is called the master tusk and this is shorter and rounder than the other one. Some elephants are trained to use their tusks and trunks to move and pick up logs.

READER 3: Elephants live in herds, in which females and young elephants stay close together. The mother chooses several other female elephants to help her look after her new baby. The adult males usually stay away from the herd. Elephants communicate over long distances with low rumbling sounds that they pick up through their feet.

ALTOGETHER: We hope that you enjoyed hearing about elephants.

    From: *Spotlight on Reading*, Routledge © Glynis Hannell 2009

Activity 24: Speed reading story

Teaching notes

Very often we want pupils to read as carefully as they can, so that they do not make unnecessary mistakes. However, many pupils get into the habit of reading word by word, which is a slow and disjointed process. Slow, fragmented reading tends to make it difficult for the pupil to understand what is being read.

In *Speed reading story*, the pupils have the opportunity to practise reading a story over and over again, aiming to increase their speed and the number of words they read correctly. This helps to build automaticity and confidence. The idea that 'practice makes perfect' is a good one to instil in pupils' minds and many pupils will be pleasantly surprised to see their speed and success rate increasing through simple practice.

Although the worksheets allow for up to six readings, the number of times a pupil reads and rereads the story is at the teacher's discretion. Usually three or four trials are plenty.

Teachers may also like to read the story to the pupil before the pupil attempts to read.

For this activity you will need to use a stopwatch to obtain an accurate record of the time the pupil(s) take to complete each read-through of each passage. To calculate the number of words read correctly, just subtract the number of errors from the total number of words in the passage.

Pupils often like to hear themselves read, so making an audio recording of the activity can be valuable.

In *Speed reading story*, the pupils have the opportunity to read meaningful language that helps them to become familiar with the structure of sentences and the flow of written language. Encourage your pupils to pause at grammatically correct pause points, such as commas and full stops.

There are no teacher's charts for this activity.

Activity 24

Speed reading story

LEVEL 1

Practise reading this. Each time you read, your teacher will put down your time and work out how many words you read correctly. See if you can read faster. See if you can read all the words correctly! What is your record?

Freddo gets a bath

Freddo the dog was very muddy.
Freddo had mud on his paws.
Freddo had mud on his tail.
Freddo had mud on his ears.

Dad got out the hose.
Dad got out the soap.
Freddo ran away.

Dad chased Freddo around the kitchen.
Dad chased Freddo around the hallway.
Dad chased Freddo into the garden.
Dad chased Freddo around the roses.
Dad chased Freddo around the trees.

Freddo ran into the fishpond.
Freddo was soaking wet.
'There,' said Dad, 'you did get a bath after all.

Readings	Time taken	Number of words	Mistakes made	Words correct
1st		90		
2nd		90		
3rd		90		
4th		90		
5th		90		
6th		90		

My record time .... My record number of words correct ....

From: *Spotlight on Reading*, Routledge © Glynis Hannell 2009

Activity 24

Speed reading story

Practise reading this. Each time you read, your teacher will put down your time and work out how many words you read correctly. See if you can read faster. See if you can read all the words correctly! What is your record?

LEVEL 2

Mr Grumble's three wishes

Mr Grumble was never happy.
He grumbled when it rained.
He grumbled when it snowed.
He grumbled when it was sunny.

He grumbled about his beautiful little cottage in the forest.

'I hate this cottage. I wish I lived in a castle,' said Mr Grumble and, would you believe it, Mr Grumble found himself in a castle!

'I hate this castle. I wish I lived in a city,' said Mr Grumble and, would you believe it, Mr Grumble found himself in a city!

'I hate this city. I wish I lived on top of a mountain,' said Mr Grumble and, would you believe it, Mr Grumble found himself on top of a mountain.

'I hate this mountain. I wish I was at home in my beautiful cottage in the forest.'

But all his wishes had run out. Mr Grumble had to live on the top of the mountain for the rest of his life.

Readings	Time taken	Number of words	Mistakes made	Words correct
1st		158		
2nd		158		
3rd		158		
4th		158		
5th		158		
6th		158		

My record time .... My record number of words correct ....

Activity 24

Speed reading story

Practise reading this. Each time you read, your teacher will put down your time and work out how many words you read correctly. See if you can read faster. See if you can read all the words correctly! What is your record?

LEVEL 3

Dolphin rescue

Josh and Kelly were having the best summer ever. Aunt Aggie had said that they were old enough to use her little wooden rowing boat, provided, of course, they stayed well within the bay.

Josh and Kelly loved the sea. Most of all they loved the sleek, smiling dolphin that came to play with them as they splashed and swam in the cool water. They called her Dorothy. Every day Dorothy would be waiting for them as they ran towards the water.

'Last day of the holidays,' sighed Kelly. 'Let's take the boat out one last time.'

So Josh and Kelly pushed the boat over the sand and into the water. Soon they had rowed out across the breaking waves into the calm water beyond. Kelly lay in the bottom of the boat with her hat over her eyes. Josh sat reading as the boat rocked gently from side to side. Dorothy swam in gentle circles around and around the boat.

'Time to go back for tea,' said Kelly after a while.

'Oh no!,' cried Josh. 'The oars, they've gone, they floated away!'

Sure enough, the oars were floating, far away. The children stood up in the boat and tried to call for help, but they were too far from the shore. They tried to row with their hands but they hardly moved at all. What could they do?

Just as they were beginning to feel really frightened, they saw an extraordinary sight. An oar was coming straight towards them! Dorothy was pushing the oar along with her nose. She had seen that they were in danger and had known just what to do. Soon Josh and Kelly had both oars back in the boat.

'Thank you Dorothy, thank you,' they called as they rowed quickly back to shore.

Readings	Time taken	Number of words	Mistakes made	Words correct
1st		299		
2nd		299		
3rd		299		
4th		299		
5th		299		
6th		299		

My record time .... My record number of words correct ....

From: *Spotlight on Reading*, Routledge © Glynis Hannell 2009

Activity 25: Speed reading sentences

Teaching notes

This is the second speed reading activity. In the previous activity, *Speed reading story*, the pupils had a continuous piece of prose to read. Now, in *Speed reading sentences*, they are presented with short sentences to read at sight.

Each sentence contains at least one frequently used word. These words are often irregular and do not 'sound out', so the pupils will need to activate their recall of whole words. The process of working against the clock and aiming for increased speed and accuracy is a very useful way to promote fluent, automatic reading. Where irregular but commonly used words are concerned this is an essential skill.

The real challenge of this activity for the pupils is that, although all the sentences are grammatically correct, none of them follows any logical pattern. It is impossible for pupils to guess what the next sentence is about; indeed it is often quite difficult for them to guess what the next word might be! This is deliberate, and is designed to develop a quick, flexible approach to reading printed words.

For this activity you will need to use a stopwatch to obtain an accurate record of the time the pupil(s) take to complete each read-through of each set of sentences. To calculate the number of words read correctly, just subtract the number of errors from the total number of words in the list of sentences.

Although the worksheet allows for up to six readings, the number of times a pupil reads and rereads the list of sentences is at the teacher's discretion. Usually three or four trials are plenty.

Teachers may also like to read the sentences to the pupil before the pupil attempts to read.

Pupils often like to hear themselves read, so making an audio recording of the activity can be valuable.

There are no teacher's charts for this activity.

Activity 25

Speed reading sentences

LEVEL 1

Practise reading these sentences. Each time you read, your teacher will put down your time and work out how many words you read correctly.
See if you can read faster. See if you can read all the words correctly!
What is your record?

1 Thank you for the toy.

2 Sam was in the pool.

3 They are as tall as giraffes.

4 When can we play in the park?

5 Can you come here on Sunday?

6 I would like to swim.

7 Dad said that we had to go to school.

8 I have some kittens at home.

9 There is a fox in the box.

Readings	Time taken	Number of words	Mistakes made	Words correct
1st		56		
2nd		56		
3rd		56		
4th		56		
5th		56		
6th		56		

My record time ....   My record number of words correct ....

Activity 25

Speed reading sentences

LEVEL 2

Practise reading these sentences. Each time you read, your teacher will put down your time and work out how many words you read correctly.
See if you can read faster. See if you can read all the words correctly!
What is your record?

1   I could jump very high on the moon.

2   You have to do that again.

3   The boy who eats the most doughnuts wins.

4   Does a crocodile really smile?

5   Do you know where birds go after dark?

6   Most people like to listen to music.

7   Every kid wanted a blue bicycle.

8   Could you walk on thin ice?

9   The father had a feather in his hat.

Readings	Time taken	Number of words	Mistakes made	Words correct
1st		62		
2nd		62		
3rd		62		
4th		62		
5th		62		
6th		62		

My record time .... My record number of words correct ....

From: *Spotlight on Reading*, Routledge © Glynis Hannell 2009   **123**

Activity 25

Speed reading sentences

LEVEL 3

Practise reading these sentences. Each time you read, your teacher will put down your time and work out how many words you read correctly.
See if you can read faster. See if you can read all the words correctly!
What is your record?

1   The children laughed when they saw my uniform.

2   There were eight fledglings in the nest.

3   The giant heaved the sack on to his shoulder.

4   The ocean was very calm after the hurricane.

5   The road turned at a sharp angle before the bridge.

6   Can you imagine how hard it is to design a helicopter?

7   There are many mysterious planets in the universe.

8   Will there be enough solar energy in winter?

9   The villain was an obnoxious character.

Readings	Time taken	Number of words	Mistakes made	Words correct
1st		75		
2nd		75		
3rd		75		
4th		75		
5th		75		
6th		75		

My record time ....   My record number of words correct ....

From: *Spotlight on Reading*, Routledge © Glynis Hannell 2009